SpringerBriefs in Psychology

Best Practices in Cognitive-Behavioral Psychotherapy

Epidemiological studies show that the prevalence of mental disorders is extremely high across the globe (World Health Organization, 2011). Moreover, and what is perhaps more concerning is the fact that, despite numerous existing evidence-based treatments for various mental disorders, more than half of those in need of specialized mental health services don't access it and/or do not have access to these treatments (Alonso et al., 2004c; Kohn, Saxena, Levav, & Saraceno, 2004; Wang et al., 2005). Thus, developing and disseminating accessible evidence-based protocols for various clinical conditions are key goals in mental health. This effort would nicely complement the efforts of the American Psychological Association (see Division 12's List of evidence-based treatments), National Institute for Health and Clinical Excellence (see NICE's Guidelines) and Cochrane Reviews (see Cochrane analyses of various clinical protocols) that identified evidence-based treatments for various clinical conditions, based on rigorous literature analyses. However, once identified, one needs a detailed published clinical protocol to deliver those treatments in research, clinical practice, and/or training (see David & Montgomery, 2011). Please submit your proposal to Series Editor Daniel David: daniel.david@ubbcluj.ro

More information about this series at http://www.springer.com/series/10143

Diana Cândea • Simona Stefan • Silviu Matu
Cristina Mogoase • Felicia Iftene • Daniel David
Aurora Szentagotai

REBT in the Treatment of Subclinical and Clinical Depression

Springer

Diana Cândea
Babeş-Bolyai University
Cluj-Napoca, Cluj, Romania

Silviu Matu
Babeş-Bolyai University
Cluj-Napoca, Cluj, Romania

Felicia Iftene
Queens University
Kingston, ON, Canada

Aurora Szentagotai
Babeş-Bolyai University
Cluj-Napoca, Cluj, Romania

Simona Stefan
Babeş-Bolyai University
Cluj-Napoca, Cluj, Romania

Cristina Mogoase
Babeş–Bolyai University
Cluj-Napoca, Cluj, Romania

Daniel David
Babeş-Bolyai University
Cluj-Napoca, Cluj, Romania

Ichan School of Medicine at Mount Sinai
New York, United States of America

ISSN 2192-8363 ISSN 2192-8371 (electronic)
SpringerBriefs in Psychology
ISBN 978-3-030-03966-0 ISBN 978-3-030-03968-4 (eBook)
https://doi.org/10.1007/978-3-030-03968-4

Library of Congress Control Number: 2018963757

This Springer imprint is published by the registered company Springer Nature Switzerland AG
The registered company address is: Gewerbestrasse 11, 6330 Cham, Switzerland

Contents

About the Authors

Diana Cândea, PhD is currently a senior assistant professor in the Department of Clinical Psychology and Psychotherapies, Faculty of Psychology and Sciences of Education, Babeş-Bolyai University, Romania, and a fellow of the International Institute for the Advanced Studies of Psychotherapy and Applied Mental Health at Babeş-Bolyai University. She is a clinical psychologist and cognitive-behavioral psychotherapist certified by the Romanian National Board of Psychologists. She is also certified by the Albert Ellis Institute, New York, as a REBT psychotherapist. Her main research interests are in evidence-based psychological interventions, self-conscious emotions, and emotion regulation.

Simona Stefan, PhD is a senior assistant professor in the Department of Clinical Psychology and Psychotherapy within BBU and a member of the International Institute for the Advanced Studies of Psychotherapy and Applied Mental Health. Her PhD thesis focused on investigating the functional/dysfunctional nature of worry in relation to other relevant factors like anxiety or irrational beliefs. Simona Stefan is also a clinical psychologist and psychotherapist and a member of the Romanian Association for Cognitive and Behavioral Psychotherapies. Her publications relate to both fundamental and applied research, her interests focusing on clinical psychology, evidence-based psychological interventions, anxiety and depressive disorders, and positive psychology.

Silviu Matu, PhD is a senior assistant professor in the Department of Clinical Psychology and Psychotherapy and a fellow of the International Institute for the Advanced Studies of Psychotherapy and Applied Mental Health at Babeş-Bolyai University, Cluj-Napoca, Romania. He is a clinical psychologist certified by the Romanian National Board of Psychologists. His main research interests are related to evidence-based psychological interventions and technology-enhanced mental health services.

Cristina Mogoaşe, PhD is a clinical psychologist and cognitive-behavioral psychotherapist certified by the Romanian National Board of Psychologists. She is also certified by the Albert Ellis Institute, New York, as a REBT psychotherapist. She is a fellow of the International Institute for the Advanced Studies of Psychotherapy and Applied Mental Health at Babeş-Bolyai University. Dr. Mogoase was involved in national and international clinical trials of the efficacy of cognitive-behavioral interventions for emotional problems in children, adolescents, and adults.

Felicia Iftene, MD, PhD, FRCP(C) is currently an associate professor at Queen's University, Department of Psychiatry, attending staff (Psychiatrist) at Providence Care Mental Health Services with additional privileges at Kingston Health Sciences Centre, and member of the Center of Neuroscience, Kingston, Ontario, Canada. She has a formal education in Psychiatry, Pediatric Neurology, Rational Emotive Behavioral Therapy, and Management of Health Services. Her main research interests are in affective disorders, schizophrenia, and child and adolescent psychiatry.

Daniel David, PhD is a professor of Clinical Cognitive Sciences at Babeş-Bolyai University, director for Research at the Albert Ellis Institute, adjunct professor at the Icahn School of Medicine at Mount Sinai, and director of the International Institute for the Advanced Studies of Psychotherapy and Applied Mental Health. His expertise is related to clinical cognitive neurogenetic sciences and evidence-based psychotherapies.

Aurora Szentagotai-Tătar, PhD is a professor of Clinical Psychology and Psychotherapy at Babeş-Bolyai University, a fellow of the Albert Ellis Institute, and a member of the International Institute for the Advanced Studies of Psychotherapy and Applied Mental Health. Her expertise is related to emotion regulation and evidence-based psychotherapies.

Chapter 1
Overview

1.1 Major Depressive Disorder: Overview

Depressive disorders are among the most prevalent and debilitating mental conditions, with major depressive disorder (MDD) as the most representative diagnostic category. The main symptoms of MDD refer to persistent negative mood and/or loss of interest and pleasure for previously enjoyed activities, as well as additional features, like loss of appetite, sleep disturbance, low self-esteem, suicidal ideation or risk, fatigue, indecisiveness, difficulty concentrating, etc. One-year prevalence rates of MDD vary between 3% and 10% in the USA (Kessler & Bromet, 2013) and 5% in Western Europe (Olesen et al., 2012), with lifetime prevalence rates higher than 15% (Kessler et al., 2003). According to the World Health Organization (WHO), MDD is estimated to become the leading cause of burden and disease by 2030 (Mathers & Loncar, 2006), and is associated with huge personal and societal costs, both directly, and through comorbidities (Greenberg, Fournier, Sisitsky, Pike, & Kessler, 2015). In this sense, in the United States, depression-related costs have increased by 21.5% between 2000 and 2015, most expenditure due to workplace costs (50%) and direct costs (45%) (Greenberg et al., 2015). The most important associated risk is suicide, with half the number of suicides being related to depressive and mood disorders, and depressed individuals having a 20-fold greater risk of suicide (Lépine & Briley, 2011). Also, MDD is highly comorbid with other mental disorders, such as anxiety disorders, substance use, or eating disorders. For instance, about 50% of depressed people in community and primary care settings also suffer from an anxiety disorder, thus making pure depression rather the exception, and not the rule (Kessler et al., 1996). In relation to substance abuse, data have shown that almost a third of MDD patients also have substance use disorders, this comorbidity leading to higher suicide risk, and greater functional and social impairment (David, Szentagotai, Lupu, & Cosman, 2008). Importantly, chronic depression is also

D. Cândea et al., *REBT in the Treatment of Subclinical and Clinical Depression*, SpringerBriefs in Psychology, https://doi.org/10.1007/978-3-030-03968-4_1

comorbid with physical medical conditions, such as heart disease and diabetes, leading to increased healthcare costs, increased medical symptom burden, functional impairment, lower treatment adherence, and a higher risk of morbidity and mortality (Katon, 2011).

Given the high prevalence and substantial costs, constant efforts have been made to address and improve the treatment of depression. Both pharmacotherapy and psychological treatments, particularly cognitive-behavior therapy (CBT), interpersonal therapy (IT), and behavior activation (BA) have been shown to be effective for depression, with similar rates of remission and similar associated risks, with CBT being the most researched form of psychotherapy (Butler, Chapman, Forman, & Beck, 2006; Cuijpers, van Straten, Andersson, & van Oppen, 2008). Although pharmacotherapy and CBT usually yield similar response rated at post-intervention, studies have found that individuals who receive CBT have lower relapse rates at 1 and 2-year follow-up compared to those who only receive medication (Vittengl et al., 2007). In this direction, recent research from the large scale CoBalT trial has shown that adjunctive CBT (i.e., to medication) leads to substantial gain retention at 46 months follow-up, thus pointing to the long term benefits of CBT (Uher & Pavlova, 2016). Nevertheless, we have to keep in mind the fact that even if CBT is effective, relapse (return of the full symptomatology before reaching full recovery) and reoccurrence (the onset of a new depressive episode following a disease-free period) are rather high, meta-analyses estimating them at 29% within 1 year, and 54% within 2 years (Vittengl et al., 2007). As for treatment response, a recent study in the UK found that conducting 18 or 20 CBT sessions for depression leads to a recovery rate of 62% (Pybis, Saxon, Hill, & Barkham, 2017). Last but not least, although effective treatments are available, many patients do not get to benefit from them, thus leaving a high individual and societal problem unsolved. For instance, in the US, the percentage of depressed patients who have ever sought treatment reaches 61.3% (Olfson, Liu, Grant, & Blanco, 2012), but it is estimated that only about 20% of them receive adequate treatment (Kessler et al., 2003).

1.2 Depression in Children and Adolescents

Depression in children and adolescents is one of the most prevalent and debilitating psychiatric disorders for this age group (Costello, Mustillo, Erkanli, Keeler, & Angold, 2003), with 12-months prevalence rates ranging from 1% in pre-pubertal children and 3% in post-pubertal adolescents (Angold & Costello, 2001), a depressive episode lasting in children and adolescents for about 9 months (Hazell, 2002). Core symptoms of depression refer to persistent low and negative mood and/or loss of interest and pleasure for previously enjoyed activities, with additional symptoms, like loss of appetite, sleep disturbance, low self-esteem, suicidal ideation or risk, fatigue, indecisiveness, difficulty concentrating, etc. In children, sad mood is often replaced by irritability.

Overall, depression poses a significant disease burden for this age group in terms of YLD (years lost because of disability), in high income countries but not only (Gore et al., 2011). Depression in youth is associated with an increased risk for other psychiatric disorders (e.g., Costello et al., 2003), with a higher risk of reoccurrence in adulthood (Harrington, Fudge, Rutter, Pickles, & Hill, 1990), being also linked to substance use (Costello et al., 2003; O'Neil, Conner, & Kendall, 2011), or difficulties in social functioning and school performance (National Institute for Health and Clinical Excellence – NICE, 2005). Suicide is the most severe complication of depression, and it constitutes the third most frequent cause of death in adolescents (Arias, MacDorman, Strobino, & Guyer, 2003). Depressed adolescents face an increased risk for attempting and committing suicide, since depression is one of the most significant predisposing factors (Harrington, 2001). Additionally, because depression in children and adolescents often comes with an atypical presentation (e.g., symptoms like unexplained headaches, abdominal pain, school refusal; Angold & Costello, 1993), many cases remain undetected and undertreated, only about 34% of depressed adolescents seeking treatment (and 23% of dysthymic adolescents) (Flament et al., 2001).

Regarding the treatment for depression in children and adolescents, several randomized control trials have found that both psychotherapy, particularly cognitive-behavioral therapy (CBT) and interpersonal therapy (IPT) and pharmacotherapy (with fluoxetine as first-line medication according to the NICE guidelines, 2005) are effective interventions, individually and in combination (Bridge et al., 2007; Vitiello, 2009). For example, the large-scale TADS (Treatment for Adolescents with Depression Study Team, 2004) found that combining medication (i.e., fluoxetine) and CBT was more effective than administering either treatments alone (i.e., as measured by the Clinician's Global Index; CGI) at the end of the acute treatment phase (TADS Team, 2007) and that it is more effective that treatments administered alone in terms of preventing suicidality on the long run (TADS Team, 2007). Also, the combination was found to be more effective than medication alone in reducing depression symptoms in adolescents with SSRI-resistant depression (i.e., as compared to switching medication) (the TORDIA study, Emslie et al., 2010). Although not all studies found that combining CBT and medication adds significantly to treatment efficacy (e.g., the ADAPT study, Goodyer et al., 2008), current mental health guidelines (NICE, 2005) recommend the combined use of SSRIs and CBT for youth depression, and advise against prescribing medication without a concurrent psychological treatment.

When it comes to particular forms of psychotherapy, a recent network meta-analysis (Zhou et al., 2015) found that only CBT and IPT outperformed control conditions at post-treatment and follow-up, the authors concluding that these are probably the most effective psychological treatments for youth depression. As it results from this analysis however, CBT is by far the most investigated treatment option for youth (e.g., 1149 randomized participants in CBT studies, compared to 344 in IPT, and fewer in the other treatment approaches). In working with youth, CBT focuses on identifying and disputing cognitive distortions, believed to be a major source of depressed mood, and on behavioral activation principles, such as activity scheduling (Verduyn, 2000). Most studies have used CBT administered in individual sessions, but data indicate that individual and group interventions obtain similar results in treating depressed children and adolescents (Weisz, McCarty, & Valeri, 2006).

Even if CBT is generally considered effective in treating youth depression, we have to keep in mind the fact that CBT effect sizes are still in the medium range (e.g., Zhou et al., 2015) with one third to one half of depressed children and adolescents still not responding to treatment (Bridge et al., 2007; Weisz et al., 2006). Therefore, finding, investigating and implementing new CBT treatment strategies for youth depression is highly warranted. In this sense, considering that Rational-Emotive and Cognitive-Behavior Therapy (REBT) has been found effective for treating depression in adults (David et al., 2008), we developed and tested a group REBT protocol aimed at reducing depression in youths, presented in the following sections.

1.3 Introduction to Rational-Emotive Behavior Therapy

Rational-Emotive Behavior Therapy (REBT; Ellis, 1957, 1962) is a form of cognitive-behavior therapy (CBT) that has at its core the appraisal theory of emotions and stress (Lazarus, 1991; Lazarus & Folkman, 1984). This theory states that emotional, behavioral and physiological responses to an event, are not directly caused by it, but rather these responses are caused by a specific type of cognitive processing, namely appraisals of the event in terms of its relevance and meaning for the individual (i.e., hot cognitions). Other forms of CBT, such as Cognitive Therapy (CT; Beck, 1976), focus on other types of beliefs that might be relevant for mental health, such as the inferences (interpretations, implications) that the individual develops in relation to the event (i.e., cold cognitions; David & David, 2017; David & Matu, 2017; David & Szentagotai, 2006). These distinctions are important from both theoretical and practical perspectives. Let us take the example of a salesman that is faced with the failure to achieve his monthly sales target. The individual might think that he has failed because he is a poor professional. This is an inference, an interpretation of the personal implications of the event. According to the appraisal and the REBT theories (David & Cramer, 2010; Ellis, David, & Lynn, 2010), the emotional response and the other associated consequences (i.e., behavioral and psychophysiological) will depend on the appraisals of this inference, and not directly on the inference. REBT distinguishes between two categories of appraisals, called beliefs, which are associated with different consequences in terms of mental health and functioning (David, 2003; Ellis & Dryden, 1997). One such category of beliefs, which are thought to be at the core of mental disorders, are *irrational beliefs*.

Irrational beliefs are defined as inflexible beliefs that do not have logical, empirical and pragmatic support. There are four types of irrational beliefs that are underlying emotional and psychological problems, according to the REBT theory:

(1) *absolutistic demands / demandigness* (DEM; e.g., "thing must happen the way I want them to happen", (2) *awfulizing* (AWF; e.g., "this is the worst thing that could happen to me"), (3) *low frustration tolerance* (LFT; "I can't stand this"), and (4) *global evaluation of worth* in relation to self, others or life (GE; e.g., "I am a bad person"; DiGiuseppe, DiGiuseppe, Doyle, Dryden, & Backx, 2013). Negative global evaluation of the self is often called *self-downing* (SD). If an individual has an irrational belief/appraisal in relation to a negative life event, then he or she is likely to experience in that context a negative dysfunctional emotion (e.g., depression) and maladaptive behavioral (e.g., social isolation) and psychophysiological consequences (e.g., lack of energy). REBT makes an important distinction between functional and dysfunctional negative emotions, and both of them can be positive or negative. Dysfunctional negative emotions, such as those in the spectrums of depression, anxiety and anger, are disabling the individual to follow his or her goals and are characteristic to mental disorders and maladaptive functioning. An irrational appraisal of a negative life event would lead to a dysfunctional negative emotion (David, Schnur, & Belloiu, 2002; David, Schnur, & Birk, 2004). Getting back to our example of the salesman, if he holds irrational beliefs related to the inference about being a poor professional, such as "I must be a good professional, otherwise I am a failure as person", then he would likely feel an emotional experience of depression and other maladaptive behavioral and physiological consequences (DiGiuseppe et al., 2013; Dryden & Branch, 2008; Ellis & Dryden, 1997).

The second category of beliefs are called *rational beliefs*, which are thought to be the hallmark of adaptive human functioning and mental health (Dryden, 2003; Ellis et al., 2010; Ellis & Dryden, 1997). These beliefs are flexible, logical and are supported by empirical facts and help the individual to reach his or her goals. The four types of rational beliefs, formulated as alternatives to the irrational ones are: (1) the formulation of own expectations as *preferences* (PREF; e.g., "I wish that things happen as I want them to happen, but I can accept that it might not turn out like this"); (2) *badness* / apprising negative events as bad, in a nuanced manner, and not as catastrophic (BAD; e.g., "What happened is very bad, but it is not the worst thing that could happen"; (3) *frustration tolerance*, which implies that the individual acknowledges the unpleasant nature of a situation, but he or she does not regards it as unbearable (FT; e.g., "I don't like this but I can stand it"); (4) *contextual evaluation* of self, other and life, which implies that the individual does not label any of these as a whole, as being either good or bad, but rather does specific appraisals of own specific behavior, the behavior of others, or apprises different aspects of life without ignoring others aspects of it (DiGiuseppe et al., 2013). The rational alternative to self-downing (SD) is called *unconditional self-acceptance* (USA), which implies that the individual is judging his or her behavior as good or bad, but at the same time acknowledges that he or she is a valuable human being. Rational beliefs are associated with functional emotions, even when the individual is confronted with negative life events, such as sadness (instead of depression), worry (instead of anxiety), and annoyance (instead of anger). These functional negative emotions do not differ from the dysfunctional ones just by intensity, instead there is a qualitative difference. Dysfunctional emotions do not interfere with the goals of the individual and are associated with more adaptive behavioral and physiological consequences. In our example of the salesman, some rational alternatives to irrational ones described above could be formulated as "I really want to be a good professional, but I can accept that I might not be one. Even if I will not become a good professional, I'm still a valuable human being". This might lead to emotions of sadness, but is less likely that he will experience depression and that he will socially isolate himself (or other maladaptive consequences).

1.3.1 The ABC Model of REBT

Clients following REBT treatments are taught the principles of this therapeutic approach using the ABC model. This model states that when the client is confronted with an *activating event* (A), the emotional, behavioral, and physiological *consequences* (C) he or she will be experiencing, are caused by the *beliefs* (B) he or she holds in relation to that event (Dryden & Branch, 2008; Dryden & Neenan, 2004; Ellis & Dryden, 1997). If the client holds irrational beliefs, then he or she is likely to experience dysfunctional consequences. This model is a simple and intuitive way of teaching the theory of REBT and offers the client a good understanding of the problems (usually the "Cs") that he or she is confronted with. Also, it gives the client an insight on what can be done to reduce the burden of his or her problems: changing the irrational "Bs" with more rational ones. The ABC model is used to formulate each of the emotional and behavioral problems the client is confronted with, although a behavioral formulation in terms of antecedents and consequences, might be used for some behavioral problems. The ABC model of REBT is used to devise monitoring forms which help the client monitor his or her beliefs and consequences in daily life.

Activating events ("As") in the ABC model could be both external (e.g., an external event) as well as internal (e.g., a physical sensation related to some disease, or a memory about a past event). For both external or internal ones, from a therapeutic perspective, is important to determine the *critical "A"*, the particular element(s) of the event that trigger the irrational beliefs of the client (DiGiuseppe et al., 2013; Dryden & Branch, 2008). Sometimes, the critical "A" might be represented by the event itself, such as getting fired from a job. But sometimes there might be some particularities of the event that are triggering the beliefs of the client. For example, the fact that he or she was fired because the company has found another employee that is better for that job. Getting more in depth, in some cases, the triggering "A" might be represented by a specific inference that the client makes about an event. For example, the inference that he is not competent might be the trigger. In such cases, some therapists (e.g., following the CT model) might be tempted to discuss about whether this inference is true or not. From an REBT perspective however, it is better to assume at the beginning that the inference is true, and try to follow the irrational beliefs that the client holds about the inference (Dryden & Branch, 2008). After these beliefs are challenged and rational alternatives are developed, the therapist might also go back and discuss whether the inferences are true or not. An activating event for a specific belief might be represented by a consequence (e.g., an emotion) of another belief. For example, a client might feel depressed because she has irrational beliefs in relation to the fact that she is feeling anger towards one of his or her parents. In this case, both initial emotion, that of anger, and the secondary one (depression), which is called a *meta-emotion*, are dysfunctional and are probably supported by irrational beliefs, but the therapist should analyze each of these sequences of the ABC model to clarify where such irrational beliefs might be present. The dysfunctional secondary emotion is often the first to be tackled in the therapeutic process (DiGiuseppe et al., 2013).

Clients might have multiple "Cs" in relation to an "A" and it is important to distinguish which are dysfunctional and which are the specific "Bs" that support them. The therapist should be aware of the fact that many clients might have trouble differentiating between different emotional states and although they were taught about the distinction between functional and dysfunctional ones, they might need additional questions and support to clarify the nature of their own emotional experiences. Moreover, patients reporting negative dysfunctional emotions in relation to an event appraised by irrational "Bs", will report at the same time some levels of negative functional emotions (David et al., 2004).

REBT states that all dysfunctional consequences have as a core belief a form of demandingness (DEM). All other irrational beliefs, awfulizing (AWF), low frustration tolerance (LFT) and global evaluations/self-downing (GE/SD) are derivated from this core belief, and are called derivative beliefs. This implies that any dysfunctional emotion that the client experience will be underlined by a core DEM in combination with one or several other derivative beliefs (DiGiuseppe et al., 2013). Depression, as a dysfunctional emotional consequence is regarded in REBT as being the result of DEM and SD in relation to some form of loss and the capacity to deal with that loss. Yet other derivative beliefs might also be present (David et al., 2002; David & Cramer, 2010). The rational alternatives, formulating expectations as preferences (PREF) and unconditional self-acceptance (USA), which would lead to an emotion of sadness, are also focused on the same content, but the difference resides in how these beliefs are formulated. Both of them reflect the desire not to encounter the loss, and acknowledge the negative nature of the loss, but while irrational beliefs are absolutistic and inflexible, rational beliefs are phrased so that they acknowledge that the turnout of the events might not be as the desired one, and that the individual is still a valuable human being, despite the lack of resources to change that state of facts.

These distinctions have some practical implications as well. Approaching a dysfunctional emotion (such as depression) using the REBT model will not lead to a positive one. Instead, the goal of the intervention is to change the dysfunctional emotion into a functional one (e.g., sadness), by changing the underlying irrational beliefs into rational alternatives (Dryden & Branch, 2008; Ellis & Dryden, 1997).

The client might also experience increases in positive emotions, as the relief of depressed mood and its transformation into sadness might allow him or her to engage in rewarding activities which become an important source of positive emotions.

1.3.2 Challenging the Irrational Beliefs in REBT

REBT practitioners use a variety of techniques to help the clients understand the irrational nature of the beliefs leading to psychological problems, and to challenge the credibility of these beliefs. This process is called disputation. Such techniques include Socratic questioning (an inquiring dialogue about the nature of the beliefs), behavioral experiments (testing the beliefs in real life situations), didactic strategies (directly teaching the client about the distinctions between the two types of beliefs), humoristic techniques (e.g., songs and other forms of art that illustrate the absurdity of irrational beliefs), and many others (see DiGiuseppe et al., 2013; Dryden & Branch, 2008), some of which will be illustrated in this book. However, each of these strategies uses one of three types of arguments that help challenge the credibility of irrational beliefs. These three main arguments are *logical arguments, empirical arguments,* and *pragmatic arguments.* Logical arguments, help the client see that the irrational beliefs that he holds are not consistent logically and thus they cannot reflect an accurate description of reality. For example, using a Socratic questioning technique, the therapist might ask his or her client "How did you come to the conclusion that only because you wish for something to happen, your wish *must* become a reality?". Empirical disputation helps the client understand that irrational beliefs are not supported by facts when they are confronted with reality. For example, using a behavioral experiment in which the client is asking another person for a romantic date, he or she might test the belief that "being rejected is awful". Pragmatic arguments are used to help the client understand that his or her irrational beliefs are not helping or are making it harder for him or her to achieve own goals. For example, making a joke during a therapy session about the fact that repeatedly stating the belief "I can't stand doing things I don't like" is surely helping the client to withstand those activities, because he or she has been doing them for so long, would make the client realize that he or she can actually tolerate thoes activities and that the irrational belief is making things more difficult (Dryden & Branch, 2008).

Disputing irrational beliefs is the key element for a successful REBT intervention. Only after the client has loosen his or her trust in these beliefs, the therapeutic process can move forward to restructure and replace them with more rational ones. In the initial phases of the treatment, the therapist might provide more input in disputing and restructuring irrational beliefs, but as the treatment progresses, the client will be guided to offer more and more input in the process until he or she becomes autonomous and independent in using the strategies he or she has been taught (Dryden & Branch, 2008; Ellis & Dryden, 1997).

References

Angold, A., & Costello, E. J. (2001). Epidemiology of depression in children and adolescents. In I. Goodyer (Ed.), *The depressed child and adolescent* (2nd ed., pp. 143–178). Cambridge, UK: Cambridge University Press.

Angold, A., & Costello, E. J. (1993). Depressive comorbidity in children and adolescents: Empirical, theoretical, and methodological issues. *American Journal of Psychiatry, 150*, 1779–1791. https://doi.org/10.1176/ajp.150.12.1779

Arias, E., MacDorman, M. F., Strobino, D. M., & Guyer, B. (2003). Annual summary of vital statistics-2002. *Pediatrics, 112*(6), 1215–1230. https://doi.org/10.1542/peds.112.6.1215

Beck, A. T. (1976). *Cognitive therapy and the emotional disorders*. New York: International Universities Press.

Bridge, J. A., Iyengar, S., Salary, C. B., Barbe, R. P., Birmaher, B., Pincus, H. A., … Brent, D. A. (2007). Clinical response and risk for reported suicidal ideation and suicide attempts in pediatric antidepressant treatment: A meta-analysis of randomized controlled trials. *JAMA: The Journal of the American Medical Association, 297*(15), 1683–1696. https://doi.org/10.1001/jama.297.15.1683

Butler, A., Chapman, J., Forman, E., & Beck, A. (2006). The empirical status of cognitive-behavioral therapy: A review of meta-analyses. *Clinical Psychology Review, 26*(1), 17–31. https://doi.org/10.1016/j.cpr.2005.07.003

Costello, E. J., Mustillo, S., Erkanli, A., Keeler, G., & Angold, A. (2003). Prevalence and development of psychiatric disorders in childhood and adolescence. *Archives of General Psychiatry, 60*(8), 837–844. https://doi.org/10.1001/archpsyc.60.8.837

Cuijpers, P., van Straten, A., Andersson, G., & van Oppen, P. (2008). Psychotherapy for depression in adults: A meta-analysis of comparative outcome studies. *Journal of Consulting and Clinical Psychology, 76*(6), 909–922. https://doi.org/10.1037/a0013075

David, D. (2003). Rational Emotive Behavior Therapy (REBT): The view of a cognitive psychologist. In W. Dryden (Ed.), *Rational emotive behaviour therapy: Theoretical developments* (pp. 130–159). New York: Brunner-Routledge.

David, D., & Cramer, D. (2010). Rational and irrational beliefs in human feelings and psychophysiology. In D. David, S. J. Lynn, & A. Ellis (Eds.), *Rational and irrational beliefs: Research, theory, and clinical practice* (pp. 99–112). New York: Oxford University Press.

David, D., & David, O. (2017). Hot cognitions. In V. Zeigler-Hill & T. K. Shackelford (Eds.), *Encyclopedia of personality and individual differences*. Springer International Publishing. https://doi.org/10.1007/978-3-319-28099-8_979-1

David, D., & Matu, S. (2017). Cold cognition. In V. Zeigler-Hill & T. K. Shackelford (Eds.), *Encyclopedia of personality and individual differences*. Springer International Publishing. https://doi.org/10.1007/978-3-319-28099-8_967-1

David, D., & Szentagotai, A. (2006). Cognitions in cognitive-behavioral psychotherapies; toward an integrative model. *Clinical Psychology Review, 26*(3), 284–298. https://doi.org/10.1016/j.cpr.2005.09.003

David, D., Schnur, J., & Belloiu, A. (2002). Another search for the "hot" cognitions: Appraisal, irrational beliefs, attributions, and their relation to emotion. *Journal of Rational-Emotive and Cognitive-Behavior Therapy, 20*(2), 93–131. http://dx.doi.org/10.1023/A:1019876601693

David, D., Schnur, J., & Birk, J. (2004). Functional and dysfunctional feelings in Ellis' cognitive theory of emotion: An empirical analysis. *Cognition and Emotion, 18*(6), 869–880. https://doi.org/10.1080/02699930341000185

David, D., Szentagotai, A., Lupu, V., & Cosman, D. (2008). Rational emotive behavior therapy, cognitive therapy, and medication in the treatment of major depressive disorder: A randomized clinical trial, posttreatment outcomes, and six-month follow-up. *Journal of Clinical Psychology, 64*(6), 728–746. https://doi.org/10.1002/jclp.20487

DiGiuseppe, R. A., DiGiuseppe, R., Doyle, K. A., Dryden, W., & Backx, W. (2013). *A practitioner's guide to rational-emotive behavior therapy*. New York: Oxford University Press.

Dryden, W. (2003). The cream cake made me eat it': An introduction to the ABC theory of REBT. In W. Dryden (Ed.), *Rational emotive behaviour therapy: Theoretical developments* (pp. 1–21). New York: Brunner-Routledge.

Dryden, W., & Branch, R. (2008). *Fundamentals of rational emotive behaviour therapy: A training handbook*. Chichester, West Sussex: John Wiley & Sons.

Dryden, W., & Neenan, M. (2004). *The rational emotive behavioural approach to therapeutic change*. London, England: Sage.

Ellis, A. (1957). Rational psychotherapy and individual psychology. *Journal of Individual Psychology, 13*, 38–44.

Ellis, A. (1962). *Reason and emotion in psychotherapy*. Oxford, England: Lyle Stuart.

Ellis, A., & Dryden, W. (1997). *The practice of rational-emotive behavior therapy* (2nd ed.). New York: Springer.

Ellis, A., David, D., & Lynn, S. J. (2010). Rational and irrational beliefs: A historical and conceptual perspective. In D. David, S. J. Lynn, & A. Ellis (Eds.), *Rational and irrational beliefs: Research, theory, and clinical practice* (pp. 3–22). New York: Oxford University Press.

Emslie, G. J., Mayes, T., Porta, G., Vitiello, B., Clarke, G., Wagner, K. D., … Brent, D. (2010). Treatment of Resistant Depression in Adolescents (TORDIA): Week 24 outcomes. *American Journal of Psychiatry, 167*(7), 782–791. https://doi.org/10.1176/appi.ajp.2010.09040552

Flament, M. F., Cohen, D., Choquet, M., Jeammet, P., & LeDoux, S. (2001). Phenomenology, psychosocial correlates and treatment seeking in major depression and dysthymia in adolescence. *Journal of the American Academy of Child & Adolescent Psychiatry, 40*, 1070–1078. https://doi.org/10.1097/00004583-200109000-00016

Goodyer, I. M., Dubicka, B., Wilkinson, P., Kelvin, R., Roberts, C., Byford, S., … Harrington, R. (2008). A randomised controlled trial of cognitive behaviour therapy in adolescents with major depression treated by selective serotonin reuptake inhibitors. The ADAPT trial. *Health technology assessment, 12*(14), 1–80. https://doi.org/10.3310/hta12140

Gore, F. M., Bloem, P. J., Patton, G. C., et al. (2011). Global burden of disease in young people aged 10-24 years: A systematic analysis. *Lancet, 377*, 2093–2102. https://doi.org/10.1016/S0140-6736(11)60512-6

Greenberg, P. E., Fournier, A.-A., Sisitsky, T., Pike, C. T., & Kessler, R. C. (2015). The economic burden of adults with major depressive disorder in the United States (2005 and 2010). *The Journal of Clinical Psychiatry*, 155–162. https://doi.org/10.4088/JCP.14m09298

Harrington, R. (2001). Depression, suicide and deliberate self-harm in adolescence. *British Medical Bulletin, 57*(1), 47–60. https://doi.org/10.1093/bmb/57.1.47

Harrington, R., Fudge, H., Rutter, M., Pickles, A., & Hill, J. (1990). Adult outcomes of childhood and adolescent depression. I. Psychiatric status. *Archives of General Psychiatry, 47*(5), 465–473.

Hazell, P. (2002). Depression in children may go unnoticed and untreated. *BMJ, 325*(7358), 229–230. https://doi.org/10.1001/archpsyc.1990.01810170065010

Katon, J. W. (2011). Epidemiology and treatment of depression in patients with chronic medical illness. *Dialogues in Clinical Neuroscience, 13*(1), 7–23.

Kessler, R. C., & Bromet, E. J. (2013). The epidemiology of depression across cultures. *Annual Review of Public Health, 34*(1), 119–138. https://doi.org/10.1146/annurev-publhealth-031912-114409

Kessler, R. C., Berglund, P., Demler, O., Jin, R., Koretz, D., Merikangas, K. R.,..., Wang, P. S. (2003). The epidemiology of major depressive disorder: Results from the National Comorbidity Survey Replication (NCS-R). *JAMA, 289*, 3095–3105. https://doi.org/10.1001/jama.289.23.3095

Kessler, R. C., Nelson, C., McGonagle, K. A., Liu, J., Swartz, M., & Blazer, D. G. (1996). Comorbidity of DSM-III-R major depressive disorder in the general population: Results from the US National Comorbidity Survey. *British Journal of Psychiatry, 168*(suppl 30), 17–30.

Lazarus, R. S. (1991). *Emotion and adaptation*. New York: Oxford University Press.
Lazarus, R. S., & Folkman, S. (1984). *Stress, coping and adaptation*. New York: Springer.
Lépine, J. P., & Briley, M. (2011). The increasing burden of depression. *Neuropsychiatric Dissease and Treatment, 7*(Suppl. 1), 3–7. https://doi.org/10.2147/NDT.S19617
Mathers, C. D., & Loncar, D. (2006). Projections of global mortality and burden of disease from 2002 to 2030. *PLoS medicine, 3*(11), e442. https://doi.org/10.1371/journal.pmed.0030442
NICE. (2005). CG28 depression in children and young people: NICE guideline. Guidance/ Clinical Guidelines. Retrieved 11 December 2012, from http://publications.nice.org.uk/ depression-in-children-and-young-people-cg28
O'Neil, K. A., Conner, B. T., & Kendall, P. C. (2011). Internalizing disorders and substance use disorders in youth: Comorbidity, risk, temporal order, and implications for intervention. *Clinical Psychology Review, 31*(1), 104–112. https://doi.org/10.1016/j.cpr.2010.08.002
Olesen, J., Gustavsson, A., Svensson, M., Wittchen, H.-U., Jönsson, B., & on behalf of the CDBE2010 study group, & the European Brain Council. (2012). The economic cost of brain disorders in Europe: Economic cost of brain disorders in Europe. *European Journal of Neurology, 19*(1), 155–162. https://doi.org/10.1111/j.1468-1331.2011.03590.x
Olfson, M., Liu, S.-M., Grant, B. F., & Blanco, C. (2012). Influence of comorbid mental disorders on time to treatment seeking for major depressive disorder. *Medical Care, 50*(3), 227–232. https://doi.org/10.1097/MLR.0b013e318241eb5e
Pybis, J., Saxon, D., Hill, A., & Barkham, M. (2017). The comparative effectiveness and efficiency of cognitive behaviour therapy and generic counselling in the treatment of depression: Evidence from the 2nd UK National Audit of psychological therapies. *BMC Psychiatry, 17*(1), 215. https://doi.org/10.1186/s12888-017-1370-7
TADS Team. (2007). The Treatment for Adolescents with Depression Study (TADS)- long-term effectiveness and safety outcomes. *Archives of General Psychiatry, 64*(10), 1132. https://doi.org/10.1001/archpsyc.64.10.1132
Treatment for Adolescents With Depression Study Team. (2004). Fluoxetine, cognitive-behavioral therapy, and their combination for adolescents with depression: Treatment for Adolescents with Depression Study (TADS) randomized controlled trial. *JAMA: The Journal of the American Medical Association, 292*(7), 807–820. https://doi.org/10.1001/jama.292.7.807
Uher, R., & Pavlova, B. (2016). Long-term effects of depression treatment. *Lancet Psychiatry, 3*(2), 95–96. https://doi.org/10.1016/S2215-0366(15)00578-7
Verduyn, C. (2000). Cognitive behaviour therapy in childhood depression. *Child and Adolescent Mental Health, 5*(4), 176–180. https://doi.org/10.1111/1475-3588.00308
Vitiello, B. (2009). Combined cognitive-behavioural therapy and pharmacotherapy for adolescent depression: Does it improve outcomes compared with monotherapy? *CNS Drugs, 23*(4), 271–280. https://doi.org/10.2165/00023210-200923040-00001
Vittengl, J. R., Clark, L. A., Dunn, T. W., et al. (2007). Reducing relapse and recurrence in unipolar depression: A comparative meta-analysis of cognitive-behavioral therapy's effects. *Journal of Consulting Clinical Psychology, 75*, 475–488. http://dx.doi.org/10.1037/0022-006X.75.3.475
Weisz, J. R., McCarty, C. A., & Valeri, S. M. (2006). Effects of psychotherapy for depression in children and adolescents: A meta-analysis. *Psychological Bulletin, 132*(1), 132–149. https://doi.org/10.1037/0033-2909.132.1.132
Zhou, X., Hetrick, S. E., Cuijpers, P., Qin, B., … Xie, P. (2015). Comparative efficacy and acceptability of psychotherapies for depression in children and adolescents: A systematic review and network meta-analysis. *World Psychiatry, 14*, 207–222. https://doi.org/10.1002/wps.20217

Chapter 2
Rational-Emotive and Cognitive-Behavior Therapy for Major Depressive Disorder in Adults

2.1 Description of an REBT Intervention for MDD in Adults – A Therapist Guide

This chapter presents an REBT protocol used for treating MDD (a previous version of this protocol can be found here: http://albertellis.org/pdf_files/rebt_depression.pdf). The protocol follows the descriptions and techniques presented in well-established theoretical and clinical guidelines for rational-emotive behavioral therapy (e.g., Ellis & Grieger, 1977; Walen, DiGiuseppe, & Dryden, 1992). This intervention was tested in a randomized control trial (David, Szentagotai, Lupu, & Cosman, 2008) and was found to be equally effective as cognitive therapy (CT) and pharmacotherapy (a detailed description will be offered in the next section).

2.1.1 *Treatment Goals*

At the beginning of the treatment an important part it is dedicated to explaining the rationale of REBT, the ADCDE model, and the goals of REBT. The intervention is guided by the following principles:

(a) A cognitive conceptualization of the problem, using the ABCDEF model;
(b) The intervention addresses the problems by focusing on the following elements: (1) behavioral activation (2) changing specific irrational beliefs, and (3) changing general irrational beliefs;
(c) A special focus on demandingness while promoting unconditional acceptance and reducing secondary disturbances;
(d) The use of a wide variety of cognitive, behavioral, and emotive techniques to change the irrational beliefs into rational beliefs;

D. Cândea et al., *REBT in the Treatment of Subclinical and Clinical Depression*, SpringerBriefs in Psychology, https://doi.org/10.1007/978-3-030-03968-4_2

(e) Use of homework assignments focused on challenging irrational thoughts and adopting adaptive behaviors.

The REBT model is focused on the irrational beliefs thought to be at the core of psychopathology, including depression: demandingness (DEM), awfulizing (AWF), low frustration tolerance (LFT), and self-downing (SD). The treatment main targets are (1) finding and changing DEM as the central irrational belief involved in depression. (2) developing unconditional self-acceptance; (3) reducing the secondary emotional problems. In case DEM is not readily recognizable, the therapist can either use direct questions to go from inferences to evaluations (i.e., inferential chaining), or can infer its presence from its derivatives (i.e., SD, AWF, LFT). However, these inferred evaluations are disputed only if the patient accepts the clinical conceptualization including DEM.

2.1.2 Session by Session Structure

The treatment consists of 20 individual 50-min therapy sessions. Therapy sessions are highly structured and should be following this format: (1) making a brief update, followed by a mood check (if the case, checking also the use of medication, alcohol and drugs), (2) making a bridge from the previous session, (3) setting the agenda, (4) reviewing the homework, (5) discussing the problem/s which was/were chosen to be approach in that session while making regularly summarizations, (6) assigning a new homework, (7) reviewing the session and feedback. The agenda is a key component for each session, giving structure and pointing the problems which will be addressed in that specific meeting. The homework it is always reviewed while the new assignment it is given at the end of the session and usually follows up a topic which was discussed in that day. The session usually covers one or two specific problems upon which both the therapist and the patient have agreed.

2.1.2.1 The Initial Phase (Weeks 1–4, Bi-Weekly Sessions)

Session 1 and 2

1. Objectives:
   - to socialize the patient with the therapy process
   - to socialize the patient with the cognitive conceptualization
   - to build an adequate therapeutic alliance

2. Main targets of the intervention:
The first 1–2 sessions are focused on the following elements:

- **Assessing the severity of depression and the underlying etiopathogenic mechanisms.** After the nosological diagnostic is established (it should be finished before this stage), patients are asked to complete measures of symptoms severity and also hypothesized causal mechanisms such as irrational beliefs in order to identify points of intervention with potential for change.

- **Education for the psychotherapy process and REBT, in particular**. At the beginning of the intervention patients are presented with the most important characteristics of the psychotherapy process. This psychoeducational part is meant to socialize the patient with the basic rules of therapy (e.g., scheduling, confidentiality, role of homework etc.). An important aspect that should be discussed is the fact that in psychotherapy the patient has an active role, thus in order to make improvements his full commitment is required. Also, it should be acknowledged that change takes time and practice. The goal of REBT is to change irrational beliefs, which have become habitual ways of thinking, into rational ones. In order to form a new mental habit, there should be emphasized the need to exercise this new style of thinking. One important way to accomplish that is by engaging in the homework assignments (see Box 2.1 for details). Also, socializing the patient with the therapy model may generate a change by normalizing his experience and this can improve the outcome of the therapy.

Box 2.1 Keys to a Successful Homework

Homework it is an essential ingredient of a successful therapy. Homework acts as a bridge between the therapy session and the client's everyday life and is the method by which in-session work is applied and generalized to tackle real-life situations. Usually the homework provides opportunities for the patient to monitor his mood or behavior (e.g., through monitoring forms), to educate himself (e.g. through bibliotherapy materials), to dispute irrational thinking and build alternative rational beliefs, and to experiment with new behaviors. There are different types of assignments. The ongoing ones (e.g., mood monitoring, behavioral activation, bibliotherapy etc.) can be assigned throughout the entire process, while others are used as a practice for issues discussed during a specific stage of the therapy (e.g., acting "as if", practice assertiveness etc.). Also it is recommended to use homework tasks which are individualized, designed especially for the problems of a particular patient.

Usually patients are willing to do the homework, however there are cases when this process it not that easygoing. In order to increase the likelihood of a successful homework there are several aspects that should be carefully approached, each of them are discussed in detail below (Beck, 1995; Dobson & Dobson, 2009; Garland & Scott, 2005).

1. *Tailor assignments to the individual.* When assigning a homework the therapist should take into consideration the individual characteristics of the person, for example her willingness to do the homework, her writing and reading abilities, her cognitive abilities and also her living environment and

(continued)

Box 2.1 (continued)

other practical constraints (e.g., when and where she can do the homework). Both the therapist and the patient should agree upon the assignment which should be in accordance with: (a) the goal of the session, (b) the overall goals, (c) the case conceptualization, (d) the severity of the patient's problems, and (e) the stage of the therapy. At the beginning of the therapy, usually, the therapist is the one suggesting the homework, while the work progresses the patient is encouraged to take the lead (e.g. "now that we discussed the problems that you have with your husband, what you think would be helpful for you to do as a homework this week?"). It seems that patients who use to set their own homework are more likely to continue doing so when therapy is over and this might prevent relapses.

2. *Provide a sound rationale.* The likelihood to comply with homework assignments increases when the patient understands the reason for doing them. For example, when introducing the monitoring form the therapist can use the following introduction: "Do you think that would be helpful for us to better know when you feel especially depressed? This might help us see what your thoughts are in that specific moment." Initially the therapist is the one who offers the rational, but it is advisable to gradually encourage the patient to think about the purpose of the assignment. It is also important to stress the rationale for doing homework regularly. Changing one's thinking and behavior requires lots of practice, attention and effort.
3. *Set collaboratively the homework.* It is important that the therapist care to ensure that the patient not only understands the rationale for an assignment but also agrees to do it. However, it should be noticed that there are overly compliant patients who may readily agree to homework in session but fail to complete it. In this cases the therapist should more carefully prepare the patient by exploring his thoughts on these issues (e.g., "Do you think you will be able to do this assignment?", "Do you think that this is something that would help you?" etc.).
4. *Ensure that there is a mutual understanding regarding the assignment.* The therapist should make sure that the patient understand what he is supposed to do. It might be helpful to have clients paraphrase their understanding of what the homework is. Also, in the first stages helping the client to formulate and write down his homework may be beneficial (e.g., "Read therapy notes and coping cards", "Go swimming or riding the bike three times this week").
5. *Provide a choice.* If there are several ways to achieve a certain goal, use the method which the patient prefers (e.g., monitor the mood by using a phone app instead of writing them down). The perception of choice enhances the person's sense of self-efficacy and control.

(continued)

Box 2.1 (continued)

6. *Make homework a no-lose proposition.* When setting up assignments initially it is really important to stress the idea that useful data can be obtained even if the patient does fail to complete her homework. Otherwise, this experience might strengthen the patient's idea that she is a failure. Also, the patient should be prepared for a possible negative outcome. For example, when assigning a behavioral experiment there are things that might not unfold as it was expected (e.g., others reactions), so it is better to discuss in advance this potential problems because it guards against possible demoralization. Also it is important to help the person to internally attribute success and improvements due to homework adherence, as we know that depressed people tend to blame themselves for the negative outcomes and to assign success to some external and uncontrollable factors.
7. *Start homework in the session.* In the first therapy sessions, it is advisable to allow time in the therapy session for the patient to begin an assignment. By doing this the therapist might see if the homework is at an appropriate level of difficulty and also it might help him to unveil potential obstacles. Also, this may motivate the patient to do the homework while the hardest part, the start, is already done.
8. *Remember to do homework.* An important aspect that should be established from the very beginning is to invite the patients to write down what their assignments are. Also, the therapist should try to identify the proper strategies to help patients to settle in doing the homework (e.g., using sticky notes, phone reminders etc.).
9. *Anticipate problems.* In order to see which might be the potential obstacles the therapist might ask himself the following questions: (a) Is the amount of homework reasonable for this patient? (b) Is the degree of difficulty appropriate? (c) Does it seem overwhelming? (d) Does it seem logically related to her goals? (d) How likely is she to do it? (e) What practical problems may get in the way (time, energy, opportunity)? (f) What thoughts may get in the way? After covering these aspects the therapist might decide to keep the same assignment, if he thinks the patients is likely to do it, or he may switch to another homework.
10. *Integrate difficulties with homework in the conceptualization.* If the patient has difficulty doing her homework, the therapist might relate these problems to those approached in the session. For example, if the patient does his homework at the last minute, this might be related to a larger problem, namely her avoidance. Thus, the beliefs underlying this problem are tackled.
11. *Engage significant others in the tasks.* Engaging the friends and family of the patient, generally increases the likelihood of completing the homework while boosting her social relations.

(continued)

Box 2.1 (continued)

12. *Review the homework.* So that the patients to understand that homework is a vital part of therapy, the therapist should take care always to attend to homework assigned at the previous session. Even when really important issues unrelated to the homework pop up, it is still useful to spend a few minutes discussing homework or to agree to discuss it at the next session. Otherwise, the patient might think that the homework it not that important and thus their motivation for doing it might decrease. The therapist should also offer feedback and discus the accuracy of the patient's performance while stressing the importance of effort and knowledge acquired and not only the results.

- **Building adequate treatment expectation.** The therapist should build hope with regard to treatment success by discussing with the patients the advantages of learning new skills for dealing with problematic emotions and behaviors. The low self-efficacy of the depressed persons may lead them to think that they can do nothing to improve the way they feel, so offering hope will contribute to an increased commitment. A special attention should be given to adjust these expectations in accordance with what we know about the efficacy of CBT with depression. Although the purpose here is to offer hope and promote engagement in the intervention, we have to remain cautious as the response rates are around 60% for moderate to severe depression (DeRubeis et al., 2005). Also, among those who do remit, up to 40% will relapse within 2 years (Boland & Keller, 2009).
- **General conceptualization of MDD**. REBT does not use a specific explanatory model for MDD, as the core cognitive mechanisms (i.e., irrational beliefs) are considered to be transdiagnostic. In MDD irrational beliefs are related to the themes of "loss" and "helplessness" which will lead to dysfunctional emotions (i.e., depression). Together with demandingness, which is the central irrational belief, global evaluation appears to be particularly relevant for MDD, leading to a sense of hopelessness. The conceptualization integrates the identified cognitions, emotions and behaviors into a coherent structure while highlighting the relation between cognitions and emotions. This integrative framework will guide the selection of the most appropriate intervention techniques, its understanding and acceptance being an essential step in the therapeutic process. However, it should be noticed that the patient may have a different theory regarding its depression and the role of the therapist in this instance is to help the patient to be aware how this model can explain its symptoms and suggest points of intervention. After discussing the conceptualization at a general level, the ABCDEF model is introduced (see Appendix 1). This model is used to conceptualize all the specific problems that will be approached in therapy (see Box 2.2 for more details).

Box 2.2 Case Formulation/Conceptualization in REBT
Currently, most CBT therapists rely on a general conceptualization before starting the treatment unless the need is pressing to treat a client before such a formulation is undertaken. Such conceptualization is usually made using the stress-vulnerability diathesis or a theory-driven explanation specific for the disorder treated (e.g., Beck's cognitive theory for depression). In REBT the ABC framework is used to help the therapist and the clients to understand the cognitive-behavioral dynamics of the clients' target problems, and generally there are no disorder specific conceptualizations. Also, in REBT the therapist do not routinely wait to intervene on the clients' problems until having carried out a case formulation. Thus, REBT therapists tend to intervene more quickly on a client's target problem and build up a conceptualization as they go rather than structuring therapy into some specific steps (Dryden, 2009).

As the ABC model is used to conceptualize clients' problems, we present below an example on how this can be done.

"Based on our theory, the effect of the thoughts on our emotional, behavioral and physiological responses can be illustrated using the following diagram:

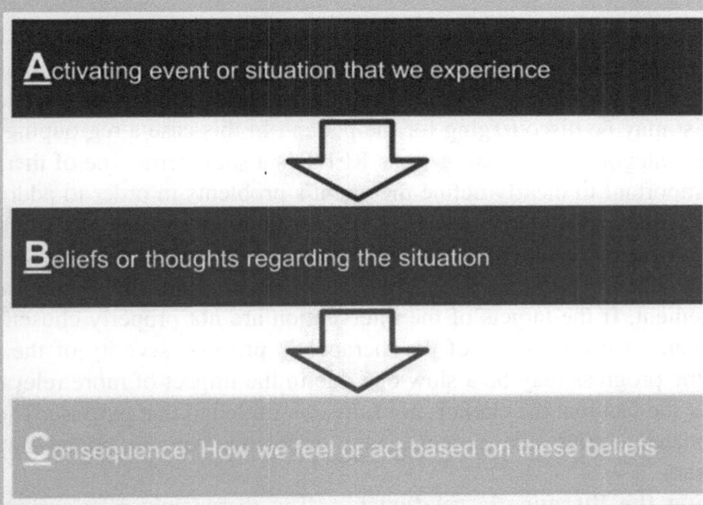

The main idea here is that not the event itself makes us feel in a certain way, but our thoughts about that specific situation. Let's take an example:

First person

A (Activating event) = A friend postpones the meeting you should have with her

(continued)

Box 2.2 (continued)

B (Beliefs/Thoughts) = 'Probably she is mad on me, nobody appreciates me, I'm a terrible person!'

C (Consequences) = Depressed, anxious

Second person

A (Activating event) = A friend postpones the meeting you should have with her

B (Beliefs/Thoughts) = 'Probably she had something urgent to do, we'll see some other time'

C (Consequences) = Neutral, maybe a bit dissatisfied

This example illustrates how, in the same situation, two people can have very different reactions depending on how they evaluate that situation based on their own beliefs and thoughts. In order to change the way you feel, in this case, to alleviate your depression, we should change those unhealthy thoughts."

- **Formulating the problem list**. The nosological diagnosis is translated into specific life problems for each patient. This personalized list usually contains up to six to eight problems upon which both the therapist and patient have agreed (a long list may be discouraging for the patient, in this case a regrouping in more general categories is preferable). As REBT is a short-term type of therapy, it is very important to clearly define the client's problems in order to address them properly in the available timeframe. Also, an important issue is the prioritization of the problems included on this list. It is recommended to begin with a central problem but an easier one, in order to produce rapid change and stimulate engagement. If the targets of the intervention are not properly chosen (e.g., in accordance with the stage of the therapeutic process, severity of the problem etc.), the progress may be a slow one due to the impact of more relevant problems or the fact that the client is not fully committed to that purpose. The list can be updated during the process, new problems can be added anytime if necessary.
- **Building the therapeutic relationship**. The therapeutic relationship is built throughout the entire process; however in the initial phase of the therapy stimulating a good alliance should be one of the therapist's main goals. The therapist should foster an environment characterized by empathy, unconditional acceptance, congruence and collaboration where together with the client, they make a team against the common enemy: the problems of the client. As up to 30–35% of the efficiency of psychotherapy is explained by the therapeutic alliance (see Lambert & Barley, 2002), it is important to address relation (see Box 2.3 for details).

Box 2.3 Therapeutic Alliance in REBT

Therapist should remind themselves about the interpersonal nature of their work and that effective REBT is not just a matter of disputing irrational beliefs. Rather, REBT is fundamentally an important interpersonal relationship. Below we discuss some specific aspects of the REBT therapeutic alliance.

The REBT theory agrees with the fact that empathy, respect and genuineness, as core conditions proposed by Rogers (1957), are solid foundations for therapeutic change, but are neither necessary nor sufficient for change to occur. REBT outlines some distinct contributions to the therapeutic relationship that may be helpful in build an adequate alliance with the patient (Dryden, 2009).

Unconditional acceptance. An important asset in building the therapeutic relationship is showing the patient that we unconditionally accept them as fallible human beings who are neither worthwhile nor worthless since they are far too complex to be given a single evaluation.

Informality. REBT therapists tend towards informality of therapeutic style although it is recommended to be formal when required. This informality might be helpful because (1) it suggest that REBT therapists take themselves and their role seriously, but not too seriously, (2) it tends to lessen the emotional distance between therapist and client without losing sight of the fact that this relationship has been established to help the client to achieve their therapeutic goals, (3) it tends to communicate therapeutic parity between therapist and client.

Humor. There is a consensus view in CBT that therapist's humor is an effective part of the therapeutic relationship, however therapist's humor is emphasized more heavily in REBT than in other CBT approaches. Humor is effective when it encourages clients to stand back and see the ridiculous in their thinking and behavior and when it promotes a determination to think and act rationally.

Some other strategies that might be used to facilitate an adequate therapeutic alliance are: (1) varying the bond with different clients; (2) varying your influence base (some clients might be impressed by your reputation while others are not interested in what you know or your reputation but in what you are like as a person); (3) varying the extent of your directiveness over the course of therapy; (4) working to facilitate your clients' learning (by using different strategies like checking clients' understanding, cover material in manageable chunks etc.); (5) encouraging your clients to undertake therapeutic tasks which are challenging but not overwhelming for them; (6) encouraging your clients to reflect on the process of REBT; (7) using a common language with your clients; (8) helping your clients to set realistic goals at different stages of the process of REBT; (9) helping your clients to commit themselves to personal change and discuss with them the necessity of tolerating discomfort in the change process (see Dryden, 2006 for more details).

3. Homework suggestions:
   - self-monitoring of negative emotions (see patient's guide);
   - bibliotherapy about depression (see patient's guide);

Sessions 2–8

1. Objectives:
   - to introduce and use behavioral activation and scheduling
   - to introduce and exercise the ABCDEF model
2. Main targets of the intervention:
   - **Behavioral activation**. Depressed persons have a low self-efficacy, negative expectations and a maximizing of the negative. Usually their behavioral repertoire is a reduced one, and thus an important step in the intervention is the introduction of activity schedule (see Appendix 2). This tool is used to track the activities of the patient during the week while countering the idea that "I can't do anything". We use this technique in order to increase the patient self-efficacy and reduce hopelessness. Also, this schedule is used to identify and increase the frequency of reinforcing and rewarding activities. Patients have difficulties in engaging in positive activities as their recall is mood-congruent. The role of the therapist is to assist the person in finding pleasurable and rewarding activities. People have the tendency to involve in those activities they think they will succeed. But depressed people have a low self-efficacy and they perceive a reduced control over the environment which dramatically influences their behaviors. These negative expectancies regarding their ability to perform different actions is due to an erroneous estimation of the results or consequences and a low control over his/her action or the environment. Also, depressed individuals anticipate that would feel much less pleasure after realizing an activity than they would actually feel. Thus, they chose not to involve in many activities fact that endorse their negative feelings and stimulate the appearance of a stable and global attributional style (e.g., "I'm no good", "I will not succeed in anything", "Nothing will change", etc.). The activity schedule can also be used to challenge these distortions. After the patient have regularly used the activity schedule, the therapist should introduce the pleasure and mastery ratings (see Appendix 3). The person is asked to make predictions about their ability to cope and enjoy the anticipated events or activities. After the event takes place, the patient is asked to re-rate their mastery of and the pleasure they felt during that specific event. The purpose is to demonstrate the effect of cognition on behavior and emotion while challenging negative expectancies.

- **Exercising cognitive restructuring**. After the REBT model was introduced in the initial sessions, the therapist begins to address each problem included on the list by using the ABCDEF model (see the patient's guide). The purpose is to work toward weakening the irrational beliefs by using a wide array of techniques (e.g., rational disputing, metaphors, songs and stories, behavioral experiments etc.). In this phase, it is also very important to highlight the common irrational beliefs which are the cause for different problems, thus helping the patient to address his/hers distortions first in retrospect and then as they arise in vivo. See Exercise 1 and 2 at the end of the chapter for a description of how to use cognitive restructuring and behavioral experiments.
- For a synthesis of techniques used in REBT and some examples of those techniques see Boxes 2.4, 2.5, and 2.6.

Box 2.4 Techniques Used in REBT

REBT uses three main categories of techniques: cognitive techniques, behavioral techniques and emotive techniques.

The cognitive techniques are specific strategies used to change or modify unhealthy thoughts in relation with a certain event. Such techniques include: scales and thoughts monitoring forms, cognitive restructuring role plays, downward arrow technique, disputing, guided imagery, "as if" experiments, coping cards and graphics, etc. In REBT the most used cognitive technique is cognitive restructuring using disputation (see the patient's guide for an exemplification and Dryden & Branch, 2008 for more details).

The behavioral techniques include specific activities the patient can do in order to help him better face negative situations. Such techniques include: activity scheduling, distraction, skills training, token economy, habit reversal, exposure etc. (see the patient's guide for some examples and DiGiuseppe, Doyle, Dryden, & Backx, 2014 for more details).

The emotive techniques are meant to change the negative thoughts while using emotional means. Humor, songs, metaphors etc. are used to generate feelings that elicit and change negative thinking (see DiGiuseppe et al., 2014 for more details).

3. Homework suggestions:
   - self-monitoring mood and behaviors;
   - elaborating and executing the activities included in the activity schedule;
   - cognitive restructuring using the ABCDEF model (see patient's guide) for problematic real-life situations;
   - behavioral experiments testing their irrational beliefs.

Box 2.5 Metaphors

Therapy metaphors use a story or illustration to see alternative ways of looking at something. Metaphors capture concepts and ideas in a way that it resonates with a person which can make a point more memorable, and help the person to make positive changes. Find below a few examples of metaphors which can be used with depressed people.

A metaphor which can be used to illustrate the impact of depressogenic thinking is that of "blinders" that are put on a horse to limit its range of vision. When people are depressed it is like if they are wearing blinders, all they can see is what is straight ahead. Depression leads people to see only what is straight ahead of them, all of which seems negative and distressing. A similar metaphor is that of wearing black glasses: when people are depressed it is as if they are wearing glasses whose lenses are covered with black paint. The information they receive from their environment passes through these lenses. So, they tend to view their experiences in a very dark, negative way.

A metaphor which can be used to illustrate the processes of identifying and modifying thoughts is that of mind as a platform. First, the clients are told to imagine that thoughts are the trains that pass through a station. The first thing they had to do is to learn to examine each train before trying to jump aboard in one of them. They should notice each train that comes into the station, some trains are continuing their way without stopping, other are pausing for a while and then go further, other are stopping there for a longer period before starting again towards their destination. This metaphor highlights the noticing of thoughts. In an extension to the metaphor, the client is instructed to change his role from train-spotter to rail inspector. Now the client's job is to examine data on trains' performance, perhaps by checking the mechanic components, the route programs, or by requesting surveys to be conducted or interviewing some passengers. The client should weigh up the evidence and determine whether the train is acceptable, or if is in need of updating, rescheduling, or complete cancellation.

Box 2.6 Humorous Songs

Humorous songs can encourage people to challenge and not taking their negative thoughts too seriously. See below two examples of rational humorous songs:

1. An REBT humorous song which is an anti-depression ditty:

   (Tune: "The Band Played On," by Charles B. Ward)

   I'M DEPRESSED, DEPRESSED!

   When anything slightly goes wrong with my life,

(continued)

Box 2.6 (continued)

I'm depressed, depressed!
Whenever I'm stricken with chickenshit strife,
I feel most distressed!
When life isn't fated to be consecrated
I can't tolerate it at all!
When anything slightly goes wrong with my life,
I just bawl, bawl, bawl!

2. A song that is consider to be helpful for people to approach their secondary symptoms, such as their depression about their depression:

   "*When I am so Blue*", written by Dr. Albert Ellis to the tune of "The Beautiful Blue Danube" by Johann Strauss, Jr.:

When I am so blue, so blue, so blue,
I sit and I stew, I stew, I stew!
I deem it so awfully horrible
That my life is rough and scarable!
Whenever my blues are verified,
I make myself doubly terrified,
For I never choose to refuse
To be blue about my blues!

These songs can be actually viewed as cognitive, emotive, and behavioral techniques: "Cognitively, in that they usually satirize and attach a major irrational belief. Emotively, in that they are musical and rhythmical, since they weld evocative well-known tunes to expressive humorous lyrics. Behaviorally, in that they are designed to be sung again and again by self-disturbing individuals, until the singers internalize the philosophies of these songs and begin to think and feel more rationally" (Ellis, 2002, p. 76).

2.1.2.2 Middle Phase – (Weeks 5–8, Bi-Weekly Sessions)

Sessions 9–16

1. Objectives:
   - to restructure irrational beliefs and consolidate rational beliefs;
   - to use in vivo restructuring in real-life situations;

2. Main targets of the intervention:

   The middle phase of the treatment includes sessions 9–16 and in this stage the therapist is:

   - **Working toward strengthening the patients' rational beliefs** while weakening the maladaptive beliefs; this work continues throughout the entire process. At this stage the client should be able to dispute his own beliefs, the therapist's role is to guide him;

- **Helping the patients to see the links between problems**, and the underlying irrational beliefs, thus aiming to change core beliefs. At this stage, the patients know which their cognitive vulnerabilities are (e.g., self-downing beliefs related to romantic relationship) and how to deal with them in a difficult situation (e.g., during a fight with the partner). New thinking patterns and behaviors are practiced in vivo in a variety of situations in order to become automatic.

3. Homework suggestions:
   - use the cognitive conceptualization (ABCDEF model) to deal with in vivo negative emotions;
   - shame-attack exercises (the person acts deliberately in a "shameful" way with the purpose of learning how to accept and tolerate the associated discomfort, e.g. wearing weird clothes, singing on the bus, making jokes with strangers etc.).

2.1.2.3 The Final Phase (Weeks 9–12, 1 Session Each Week)

Sessions 17–20

1. Objective:
   - to generalize rational thinking in new real-life situations
2. Main targets of the interventions:
   The last four sessions (sessions 17–20) are focused on:
   - **Preparing the patients for becoming their own therapist** by helping them to understand how they can use all they have learned in therapy without the help of the therapist.
   - **Discussing dependency problems and relapse prevention**. Patients are further trained in identifying difficult situations while using rational thinking to deal with them. Also, patients are trained on how to recognize the signs of relapse in case it occurs (e.g., feelings of depression and hopelessness). Some patients may be willing to continue the therapy because they don't think they could deal with their problems without specialized help. To prevent this, the preparation for ending the therapy should be carefully approached by fostering patient's self-efficacy on this matter while rehearsing the previously learned strategies and discussing potential problematic situations.
3. Homework suggestions:
   - continuous use ABCDEF model in real-life situations;
   - identifying future problematic situations.

2.2 A Clinical Trial Testing the Protocol for MDD in Adults

This protocol was tested in a randomized control trial investigating the efficiency of REBT compared with CT and pharmacotherapy (David et al., 2008). The study included 170 patients (113 females and 57 men) with major depressive disorder as their primary diagnosis following the DSM-IV, by using the Structured Clinical Interview for DSM-IV (SCID; First, Spitzer, Gibbon, & Williams, 1996) and scored at least 20 on the Beck Depression Inventory (BDI; Beck, Rush, Shaw, & Emery, 1979), and 14 or higher on the 17-items of Hamilton Rating Scale for Depression (HRSD; Hamilton, 1967). The exclusion criteria were: (1) a number of comorbid psychiatric disorders (i.e., bipolar or psychotic subtypes of depression, panic disorder, current substance abuse, past or present schizophrenia or schizophreniform disorder, organic brain syndrome, or mental retardation); (2) following some concurrent form of psychotherapy or receiving psychotropic medication; (3) a high risk of suicide or psychosis resulting in hospitalization. Participants were randomly assigned to one of the three study condition after matching to ensure group equivalence on the following variables: number of previous episodes of depression, presence or absence of dysthymia, gender, and marital status. The efficacy of the three treatment approaches was evaluated at post-treatment and at 6-month follow up (with both BDI and HRDS). The results indicate that REBT, CT, and pharmacotherapy are equally efficient at post-treatment for patients suffering from major depressive disorder. However, at 6-month follow-up, REBT and CT seem slightly more efficient than pharmacotherapy, but only REBT was significantly better than pharmacotherapy (only as assessed by the HRSD). Also, both psychological intervention were associated with a reduction in the proposed mechanisms of change: (a) automatic thoughts, (b) dysfunctional attitudes, and (c) irrational beliefs (Szentagotai, David, Lupu, & Cosman, 2008). Also, at follow-up, a change in implicit demandingness appeared to be more strongly associated with reduced depression symptoms and relapse prevention.

2.3 Practical Examples and Exercises for the Therapist

Exercise 1. An Example of How to Use Rational Disputation During the Session

Florence is 21 years old and she is currently a second-year student in English literature. She came to the therapist office after failing to show on several exams during the winter term and failing some others where she did go. A close friend with whom she talked about her problems recommended her to go and see a psychotherapist. She did not mention any of her psychological and academic problems to her parents or other family members. Clinical assessment revealed a diagnosis of major depressive disorder with no other clinically significant comorbidities. The patient has already been familiarized with the REBT therapeutic approach, the ABC model, the link between thoughts and emotions, and has been using an activity schedule for 2 weeks. She has also been monitoring her thinking patterns for the last week. This is the fourth session in which the therapist plans to introduce her to rational disputation and the ABCDEF model. Below is an excerpt of the verbatim transcript of the session.

Verbatim Transcript
(T = Therapist, Florence – C = Client)

T: We discussed the previous session about the ABC forms that you should fill for each moment in which you have some strong emotional response that might interfere with your goals and activities during the week. How did that go?

C: I think I did my homework. I mean, I did fill them as we discussed. Here they are. You can have a look at them [the patient hands the ABC forms to the therapist].

T: Thank you. I will review them but let me ask you first if there was anything that popped out. I mean, was there any particular moment that you felt strongly distressed?

C: Yes, there were a few. It wasn't my best week. I filled a form for each of these events.

T: I am sorry to hear that you felt bad… Where there any events in which you felt depressed that you would like to discuss in particular? I think it might be useful for our session to start from those. I would like us to discuss in depth about how you might get yourself to feel less disturbing emotions by looking at your thinking in those moments. What do you say?

C: If you think that it might help me, I agree.

T: Let us give it a try. Can you think to such a moment and point me the form? Have them. [The therapist hands back the ABC forms to the client]

C: Ok, so there was this particular event [the client is looking through the ABC forms] when one of my colleagues said that my idea about how to interpret the text we read during the literature seminar is so obvious that it makes the text look ugly and flat. This is the form.

T: Ok, let me see that. [the therapist is looking at the form]. I see you wrote here about the negative remark of your colleague. And that you felt very disappointed about yourself and depressed. You wrote down your thoughts which were: "I have no creativity. I will never be a copywriter. My professional life will be terrible".

C: Yes, something like that.

T: What do you mean by "something like that"? I mean, this is what you wrote down, right?

C: Yes, but I am not sure these were my thoughts. I had a lot of thoughts after that, and I felt very bad because of what my colleague said. I wrote down what I felt and what I thought a bit later, when I had some space, but I am not sure I got it all.

T: I see. I think is fine, it can't be perfect. I mean, it might not reflect all of your thoughts, and I think you can get better with this with more exercise. I would like to spend some time discussing about this event. What do you say? Would that be

OK? It might help you structure your way of looking at your thoughts and find the most relevant ones.

C: I guess so.

T: Good. Let us start with what happened. The "A" from the ABC model.

C: OK.

T: What was it about this particular event that made you in the end feel so bad? Was it the fact that your colleague did not like your interpretation of the text, how he said that, or the tone of his voice? What he actually said? Or was it related to the fact that it was this particular colleague?

C: I don't know. I mean, kind of all of them.

T: OK. So, we have this colleague who is somewhat important to you? Right?

C: Kind of.

T: Why is that the case?

C: She is a good student. Marta, is a very good student and a very creative one. She seems so smart and so talented and easy going with other people.

T: Do you like her particularly? Is she a model for you or a friend, or I don't know…

C: I think she is a smart and talented student like I would like to be. I think she will make a great career as a copyrighter. I care about what she says. If she finds that my interpretation of the text is so flat, then probably it is.

T: I see that. So, there is this colleague you appreciate, and she makes these negative remarks on your ideas and your creativity. You think that you will be a terrible copywriter and that makes you feel bad. Tell me more about how you felt just after these thoughts came to your mind.

C: I felt very sad and useless.

T: Would you say that it made you feel depressed?

C: Yes. Very depressed.

T: What did you do when you felt so depressed?

C: I just got stuck in my mind thinking about how awful my life is, or is going to be, and I could not concentrate anymore. I left early from the second part of the seminar.

T: It really affected you…

C: Yes, it did.

T: I think that being sad after some relevant person criticizes your work or ideas, it is somehow expected. But would say that the way you felt actually interfered with your goals? You did want to follow the seminar, right?

C: Yes, I did, but I couldn't, because of the way I felt.

T: Ok, so this is the kind of emotion for which we would like you to have more control over it. I mean it is fine to be sad when something like this happens, but getting away from your goals because of that, is not helpful.

C: I know. I just don't know how to do that.

T: Hmm… Let get back to your thoughts. It is interesting how you jumped to the conclusion that you are going to be a terrible professional based on what your colleague said… but I will leave such a discussion for another time. I would like to focus on something else at this point.

C: OK. What?

T: Do you recall which thoughts we should look to help you change the way you feel? To make you feel healthier emotions?

C: The irrational thoughts.

T: Right. What irrational thought made you feel depressed in this situation?

***C: The fact that I thought I will be a terrible copyrighter. This is a type of awfulizing as you told me.**

T: It might be. But I would like to get to what I think might be at the core of the problem in this case.

C: OK, what is it?

T: Let me see if I got it well. A colleague whose opinion you value makes a negative comment on your ideas. You inferred from this that you will be a bad professional, a copyrighter with no creativity or that you will never get to be a copyrighter in the first place.

C: Yes, like this.

T: But let me ask you what does it mean to you to be a bad professional? You said earlier that your life is going to be awful? Is it truly like this?

C: Yes. I mean if I can't be what I want to be, if I can't achieve my own goals, what is the purpose of all this? Why even put the effort then?

T: Aha. And what about yourself? Does this matter for how you see yourself? I mean, how would you see yourself if you don't achieve these goals?

C: A failure. I would be a total failure.

T: Does the remark of your colleague makes you think that you are a failure?

C: Kind of.

T: OK, but why do you think you should become a creative copyrighter in the first place?

C: What do you mean? This is what I want for myself. This is why I started studying English literature in the first place.

T: We all have many goals for ourselves that don't become reality, but not all of us feel depressed because of that.

C: Yes, we all have such goals. I do too. But this one, must happen. This is the most important one for me. Or at least one of the most important.

T: OK. Let us think about what you said for a minute. Let me rephrase that for you. "This is an important goal and must happen, otherwise my life will be awful and I will be a failure". What do you say about this?

C: That sums it up quite well.

T: Yes, but just try to look through the lenses of what I have taught you about the thinking patterns that make us feel depressed.

C: I am thinking irrational.

T: Yes. But we can do something about it.

C: What?

T: We can find more rational ways to think about this. Let me first ask you a question. How many of your colleagues want to become a successful and creative copyrighter?

C: Almost all of them.

T: And how many of them are going to actually become one. I mean, think realistically? Is this a profession where everybody makes it to the top?

C: No. It is very hard to get there. You have to be very good and have at least some luck.

****T: OK. This means that almost all of our colleagues want to become copywriters, but at the same time, very few of them will actually become one. Does this mean that their lives are all going to be awful and they are all failures? If so, perhaps they all should feel depressed as well.**

C: No, they are not failures. And I don't think they are depressed. Or at least they don't seem depressed.

T: They are not failures you say. Why not? If this is an important goal for them. I imagine that they all value their career perspective.

C: Because they are good people, and there are other things in life than just career.

T: They are people. Just people. Sometimes they are successful, sometimes not. And yes, life is more than about one thing. Whatever is that thing. Career or anything else.

C: I see…

T: Even if we don't succeed in something important, that does not make us a failure. No matter what that thing is.

C: I understand now.

T: You said your life is going to be awful. Is that really so? I mean, can you imagine a life that is worse than the one in which you are not a copywriter?

C: A life that is worse than that? I don't know…

T: Think about it. What can make your life being worse?

C: Being a copywriter and living alone, without anyone to care about you, and to care about.

T: Good. That is a good start.

C: What do you mean?

T: Can you imagine something worse than that?

C: Worse? Is that even possible?

T: I would bet so.

C: OK. Let me think… Perhaps not having a job. I mean any job, to support myself.

T: Yes. And we can go even further. I think you got the idea.

C: Yes. I think I did.

T: Tell me, which is it?

C: There are always worse scenarios than the one that you imagine or fear.

T: Far worse, actually.

C: Yes, I agree with you.

T: Let me ask you one more important think.

C: What is that?

T: You said this goal must happen. We discussed about what could be the consequences if it does not happen. You are not a terrible person and your life is not going to be awful. But let us turn back to why it must happen?

C: Because I think. This is what I want.

T: So it must happen because you want so?

C: Yes, something like this. Now I see. I recall from our last session that you taught me that is irrational to have life goals that must happen.

T: Yes. But I would like you to see with me why is it irrational.

C: OK. I am following.

*****T: This idea has a logical fallacy. If you wish something, does it really have to happen? If anyone on this planet want something really badly, does this mean that it has to happen? Just because they want so?**

C: Not necessarily. But if she or he works hard enough, he might get that thing.

T: Yes, she or he might get it, but it also might not. Nothing happens just because we want so. And even if we put our best efforts, it still might not happen. And we are not terrible persons because of that… and so on.

C: OK, I think I understand. The “issue” here is the fact that I am telling myself that I must become a copyrighter. Not that I wish for that.

T: Yes. Exactly. You can wish for whatever you want, but you should also understand that it might not happen.

C: It makes sense to me now. How should I do all of this in real life? How should I think about my problem?

T: You tell me. Based on what you have learned, how could you think about your wish of becoming a copywriter so that you could feel better in your situation. Let’s take the point where we started from, your colleague making those negative comments.

C: I will make a try… Even if I don’t become a copywriter, there are other things that are important in life, and I still can have a good life after all.

T: That sounds good. You can emphasize your wish for becoming a copywriter.

C: I wish I become a successful copywriter but if that does not happen, I can still have a good life.

T: That sounds even better. I would add the idea that your worth, as a person, does not depend on your achievements.

C: One more try. I wish I become a successful copywriter but if that does not happen I can still have a good life and I am a valuable person no matter my achievements.

T: I think that is quite good. I think you got the idea. Let us try another example and see how it works.

Tasks

1. What is the activating event (A) for the emotional problem discussed during the session?
2. Which are the irrational beliefs that Florence has in relation to that event?
3. Would you say that “a terrible copywriter”, as present in the text marked with the symbol “*” is a form of awfulizing, as in the REBT model?
4. Identify what type(s) of disputation is(are) being used in the line marked with the symbol “**”.
5. In the line marked with the following symbol “***”, the therapist is using a logical strategy for disputation. How would you address the same cognitions by using a pragmatic disputation? What questions would you ask?

Exercise 2. An Example of How to Plan an Behavioral Experimentation

Alexander is a 32 years old high school professor, teaching mathematics. He is married and has two children. The first child is 7 years old and is now in primary school. The second child is just one and a half years old. His wife, also a high school professor, is in maternity leave, taking care of the baby. Alexandre has being diagnosed with depression 3 months ago and has been following an REBT treatment since then. He has made good progress in treatment. His main practical problems have been related to supporting the family, given that his wife has a much lower income while in maternity leave, so that he is now required to give private lessons. He has also been taking care of his older son, taking him to school, spending time on homework, and taking him to various extracurricular activities. Alexander has been feeling overwhelmed by the responsibilities and feels that his wife has not been supportive with him. Before coming to therapy, a mother has filed a complaint to the school management about the poor teaching that Alexandre has been doing in the classroom where her child was a student. Alexander's irrational beliefs underlying his symptoms of depression, as revealed in therapy, are related to his demandingness and self-downing for supporting his family, and those for being poor as a teacher. Also, he has beliefs of demandingness, negative global evaluation and awfulizing about being a loving and carrying husband. In this session, the client and the therapist identified the following belief "I must always help my wife when she is in need, otherwise I am a bad and careless husband" and are now planning for a behavioral experiment.

Verbatim Transcript

(T = Therapist, Alexandre – C = Client)

T: We have this belief which states that you must always respond to every request for help from your wife in order to be a good husband. How can we test this in real life?

C: You mean to test it with my wife?

T: Given that this belief is in relation to your wife, I would suggest so. The idea is to have you act against this belief to see if it holds up.

C: To act against it? To do something that is contrary to what I would regularly do?

T: It might imply this as well, but not necessarily contrary to. The focus here is on what would you do based on this belief you have, and try to act differently. We have to think of a context that is relevant for this.

C: That is easy. My wife always asks me to help her. I have many contexts to try.

T: [courtesy laugh]. Ok, let us pick one of them.

C: How to choose? I am not sure how…

T: Try to recall a time where you felt bad because you thought that you are not helping enough. In which your belief, "I must respond to my wife's requests for help, otherwise I am a bad husband", becomes triggered. We have to think about such a moment. We can start from one of the situations that we have already discussed about. But it has to be something that tends to repeat itself.

C: OK, let me think about it… [Pause]. I do get this feeling often in the evening, when I review my agenda for the next day and I try to prepare something for the classes or the private lessons. This is a time then my wife might ask me to help her with something, like taking care of the baby while she takes a bath or she is making a phone call. If I don't help her out, I get the feeling that I am selfish.

T: Do you also get the thought that you must help her?

C: Yes. Sometimes I postpone her request and I tell her that I will help later.

T: Do you help her in the end?

C: Yes. But I get the feeling that I am being a selfish person while I finish my work.

T: OK, I understand. It might be a good situation for our experiment.

C: But don't you think that this is bad idea? I mean, it would be very rude to tell her that I would help her, and then not doing it.

T: This would be rude, but still not catastrophic. And it would not make you a bad husband. Still, I am not suggesting telling her that you would help, and then not helping her. We can think of an experiment that does not imply making a promise that you plan not to keep it. Even though that might be an interesting experiment as well.

C: Interesting? Really? How comes that?

T: Don't get me wrong here. Think about what you have learned the last sessions. Sometimes we do things that might seem selfish or rude. That is part of being a human. I don't encourage you to do so. But if you do it, you are still a valuable human being.

C: Yes, I know. Then how should I do it?

T: Think about it. What is this belief telling you and why is it irrational? This is what we want to challenge through the experiment.

C: OK. It is irrational because I think I always must help. And because it tells me what I should do in order to be a good husband and person.

T: Yes. How can we test if this belief really holds?

C: I should not respond to the request of help and see how it feels.

T: Yes…

C: To see if that really makes me a bad husband.

T: Perfect. What would this mean in the situation you chose earlier?

C: To say to my wife I can't help her, even though she needs my help.

T: Or at least even though she has requested it.

C: Yes, even though she has requested it.

T: Can we plan this?

C: What do you mean?

***T: I think that as a first time is better if we plan this exercise. It will make it somehow easier for you. It will also make it somehow safer. Next time you can improvise more.**

C: OK. You are asking when I can turn away my wife's request for help?

T: Not exactly like that. But let us make a plan about how you could do it and see how it might go.

C: I can do it tomorrow. The day after, I have a day full of private lessons that I should prepare for. I can do my work and turn off anything that she asks.

T: It does not have to be anything. We have to be flexible. If some kind of emergency emerges, something that is important, you might want to help. But smaller, everyday stuff, you might refuse to do it. Or at least say that you will be able to help only after you finish all of your work.
C: OK. But if she asks me something that takes just a moment?
T: For the sake of the experiment, I would turn down that request as well. You will see how to deal with this after this experiment.
C: Should I tell her in advance that I will not be able to help her?
T: Does she interrupts you even when she knows that you are busy?
C: Yes. I think it does not make a difference for her.
T: OK. Then, it does not make a difference either. You can choose if you want to tell her or not that you will be working.
C: I think I will not tell her.
T: Good. And how will you do it? What exactly are you going to tell her?
C: I will tell her that I have something important to work and that I will be able to help her only after I finish… and that it will take me a while.
T: What if she insists?
C: I will re-iterate that is something important and that I can help her later.
T: OK. You do not have to be rude. You can be assertive.
C: OK. I will try not to yell or something.
T: Great. Let me ask you about the consequences. What it might happen if you do so?
C: What do you mean? You are asking how she might react?
T: Yes…
C: I think she will insist and tell me that it would only take me a couple of moments.
T: OK. But afterwards? Do you think she might put some blame on you?
C: I am not sure. She might do so later after the children are in bed. Before we sleep or something.
T: What is a likely negative scenario?
C: She might tell me that I am selfish and that she needs my help because she feels exhausted.
T: How would you react to this?
C: Normally I would feel bad about this. It would start my depressive thinking.
T: In a situation when she tells you this, would you try to ask her to forgive you or would you try to compensate for this?
****C: Yes. To feel better, I would promise her that it would not happen again. I would also try to make things up the next day**.
T: Aha… I think, for the sake of the experiment, you should try not to do these things. Do you know why?
C: Because it would be a way to act based on the same belief, right?
T: Exactly. Great. I think you are quite prepared. Put it into action. If depressive feelings get to you when you do this, try to challenge them. As you have learned.
C: Yes. It is not the end of the world and I am not a bad husband even if I might not be there for her every time.
T: Yes. Sometimes we act against what others expect from us, and that does not make us bad. We are humans and this is normal.

C: … [Pause]. Yes, we are.
T: How do you feel about this? About the experiment?
C: It does not feel easy, but I am willing to try it.
T: I can understand how you might feel. I am glad that you have the courage to try it… [Pause]. Do you think we can move to the next topic on our agenda?
C: Yes, of course.

Tasks

1. What is the rationale for the explanation given by the therapist marked with the symbol "*". Why the therapist thinks that the behavioral experiment needs to be planned and to be safe?
2. Think about the behaviors described by the client in the line marked with the symbol "**". Try to analyze this from the perspective of the ABC model of REBT. How are these behaviors helping the patient feel better? Think about the long-term consequences.
3. Try do devise a behavioral experiment about another of Alexander's beliefs, namely: "I must always succeed in my work, otherwise I am a bad professional and I can stand such a situation". How would you approach this belief in relation to his work as a high school teacher?

2.4 Description of an REBT Intervention for MDD – A Patient Guide

2.4.1 Aim of the Manual

The aim of this manual is to teach you various skills that will help you to manage your depressive symptoms or any other related difficulties. This manual will teach you about REBT and how you can use its principles and techniques to alleviate your mood. Research shows that up to 75% of patients receiving REBT will experience improvements in depressive symptoms. By reading this manual you will find out what to do to be less depressive, more energetic and how to deal with any disturbing symptoms. The skills which you will learn will help you to better manage emotional distress.

2.4.2 What Is Depression?

Depression (major depressive disorder) is a common and serious medical illness that negatively affects how one feels, thinks and acts. Depressive symptoms are not experienced in the same way by all individuals, while some may feel always fatigued and have serious difficulties in concentrating; other may feel particularly irritable without any clear reason. Depression affects the way the individual eats or sleeps, the way that he/she perceives himself/herself or the way he/she views the world. Depression is not the same thing as a passing sadness. It is not a sign of weakness, nor a thing which would disappear if the person has enough will or strive enough. If you are depressive you cannot simply put yourself together. Without treatment symptoms can last for weeks, months and even years. However, appropriate treatment might be helpful for most people diagnosed with major depressive disorder. Many people do not look for professional help even though the big majority will benefit greatly from it. The treatment of depression is very important as this disorder is affecting you, your family and your capacity to accomplish your duties. Some individuals will hurt themselves thinking that the way they feel will never change. You should keep in mind that depression is treatable.

2.4.3 What Is Rational-Emotive Behavior Therapy?

REBT is the first type of cognitive-behavioral therapy and was created by Dr. Albert Ellis in 1955. The main assumption of REBT is that events alone do not cause a person to feel depressed, angry, or highly anxious; it is one's beliefs about the events which generated the unhealthy feelings and maladaptive behaviors. There are two categories of beliefs: (1) rational/healthy beliefs which generate functional emotions and adaptive behaviors and (2) irrational/unhealthy beliefs which generate dysfunctional emotions and maladaptive behaviors. REBT teaches you how to actively confront your irrational beliefs and how to assimilate rational beliefs which are healthier and have a positive impact on your emotional, cognitive and behavioral responses. REBT uses various techniques meant to help you feel better both emotionally and physically in order to adopt healthier behaviors. These strategies can be categorized in: (1) cognitive techniques which are used to change unhealthy thoughts in order to alleviate your mood, (2) behavioral techniques which teach you how to cope with stressful events (e.g., activity planning) and (3) emotive techniques which are also used to change negative thoughts but by using emotion strategies (e.g., songs, humor etc.).

2.4.4 Managing Depression with Behavioral Techniques

When you are depressed you may feel that you don't have energy to do anything. You may think that you will start to do some things when you will begin to feel better, but you won't start feel better if you don't do something. You can find below some strategies that may help you to get the things going.

2.4.4.1 Activity Scheduling/Planning

When you feel overwhelmed by negative thoughts and you feel tired and with not much energy left you may try to plan your daily and weekly schedule. Planning your daily and weekly schedules will help you manage better your daily activities, decrease your negative thoughts, control your level of fatigue, and most important, help you feel more in control of your life (Box 2.7).

Box 2.7 Activity Planning

You can find below several steps you can take in order to efficiently schedule your activities:

1. You can begin by writing down your weekly REBT session. Keep in mind that a session last on average 50 min and you should also allow extra time for traveling to and from the office.
2. Establish an approximate timeline for each of the 3 daily meal breaks. You may also want to include several 10–15 min snack breaks.
3. Plan at least one 30-min daily physical/recreational activity. Pick an activity that you enjoy doing, such as walking, riding the bike, or attending yoga classes. These activities are extremely helpful as they give you energy and keep your fitness at an appropriate level.
4. Make a list with all the activities you would like to complete during the day. This list should contain all the activities you are responsible for (i.e., work-related activities, daily chores etc.) and also activities you would enjoy doing. Then, you should prioritize the activities by thinking how important is for you each of those activities. You can order them by assigning a number to each of them (e.g., 1 = finishing the work assignment, 2 = doing the laundry etc.). Now schedule these activities in your calendar using Appendix 2. and make sure you have enough time to accomplish each of them. If you cannot fit in all the activities in a given day, you can postpone those you rated as less important in another day when you have more free time. Although is tempting to schedule other activities instead of resting or taking a physical/recreational activity, we recommend you not to do that as these activities are particularly important for keeping a balanced and healthy lifestyle. Try to set realistic goals; there is a limited number of things you can accomplish in 1 day. An overloaded schedule will only set you up for disappointments as it will be impossible to finish all the activities.

2.4.4.2 Distraction Techniques

This kind of techniques will help you take of your mind from the negative thoughts. You can:

(a) imagine a pleasant image; you can think of a beautiful place you have visited or you would like to visit, you can remember something beautiful that happened to you or you can picture you doing something you love.
(b) listen to relaxing songs or watch a comedy.
(c) take a break and go for a walk, focus on what you see and hear.
(d) visualize a STOP sign; every time you feel overwhelmed by negative thoughts try to imagine a STOP sign, a red one like those road signs, which will be your signal that you should stop thinking like that and try to think about something else.

2.4.5 Managing Depression with Cognitive Techniques: Mastering Your Thoughts

We may not always pay attention to our thoughts, but nevertheless they have a strong effect on how we feel and behave in response to a particular situation or event. According to the cognitive theory, it is not the event that makes us feel in a certain way, it is our thoughts that influence the way we feel and act. This idea is summarized by the following scheme:

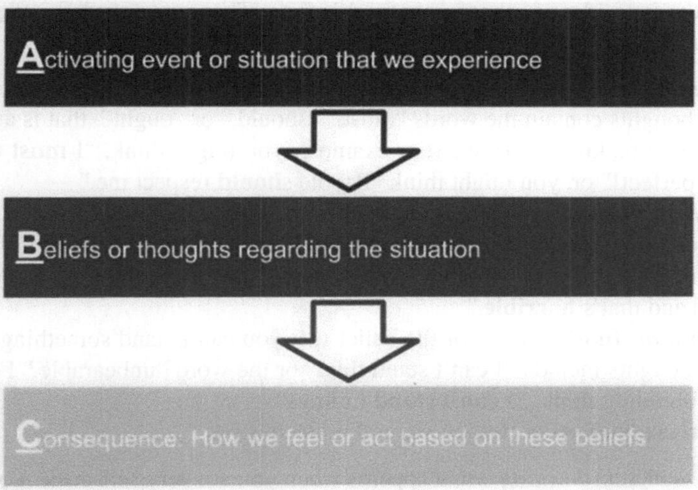

The key to changing the way you feel is changing the way you think. In order to do so, you can use the following approach: the ABCDEF form. Let's see how you can use it.

We will begin with the first box: **the A's (Activating Events)**.

In this box, you have to write about an upsetting event that you experienced today. For example: "I feel depressed because I failed at work". You should try to fill in examples that are relevant to you. An important step in making a change is to monitor the times you feel really blue and sad or when you feel exhausted. If nothing bad happened today, please make reference to the most recent negative event in your life.

Before we move on to B's, let's first focus on C's.

The **C's** box is dedicated to the **consequences** following the events.

In this box, we would like you to write the consequences of the event. There can be three types of consequences that you can experience:

- *Unhealthy negative feelings*, for example depression, anxiety, anger. You should write there the words that best describe the way you feel.
- *Maladaptive behaviors*. These are actions you do that are unproductive or harmful in some way (e.g., procrastinating, isolating yourself etc.)
- *Negative Physical Consequences*. When we experience an unwanted event there are some physical symptoms that might appear. For example, when you are into a fight with someone you may feel that your heart beats faster or you can find yourself trembling. Write down in this box physical reactions you have experienced in that specific situations.

Changing the way you feel by changing the **B's (Negative or Unhelpful Beliefs)**.

As we have already seen, and even though it may be hard to accept at first, in reality it is not the events that make us feel bad, but the negative beliefs that we hold. A first step is to identify these unhelpful beliefs. There are four big categories of negative beliefs:

- ***Demandigness*** – or the strong belief that things should be in a certain way. If your thoughts contain the words "must," "should," or "ought", that is a sign that you hold this kind of beliefs. For example, you might think, "I **must** to everything perfect!" or, you might think "People **should** respect me."
- ***Awfulizing/Catastrophizing*** – or the beliefs that the thing that happen to you is the worst thing possible. Specific words indicating the presence of this belief are "awful," "horrible," or "terrible." For example, you might think, "I had upset my friend and that's **horrible**."
- ***Frustration Intolerance*** – or the belief that you can't stand something. Look if your thoughts include "I can't stand this!" or the word "unbearable." For example, you might think, "I **can't stand** failing!"
- ***Global evaluation-*** or putting general etiquettes on:

  (a) *you* ➔ *self-downing* – that appears when you are very self-critical or beating up on yourself. Also, when you conclude that you are worthless based on a few minor things. For example, you might think, "I was too sad today to go out with my colleagues. **I'm a boring and terrible person**."

  (b) *others* ➔ *other-downing* – that appears when you are very critical or beating up others, or when you make general judgments about them based on few incidents. For example, you might think, "My wife is not helping me to feel better. **She's totally selfish and unloving**."

  (c) *Life* ➔ *life-downing* – check whether you're judging *all* of your life as terrible, just because things are not the way you wanted them to be. For example, you might think "**Life is worthless** because I am not capable of doing anything."

Negative thoughts are those thoughts that make us feel and/or behave in a negative, or unwanted manner (e.g., feeling depressed or angry). Once you have identified the negative beliefs you have about the situation, use the "B" box to write them down.

Leave away unhelpful thoughts by **Debating your Negative Beliefs- D's**.

After you recognize your negative or unhelpful thoughts, the next step is to fight with them by **debating** or challenging them. How you can do this? By asking some of the following questions.

(a) You may ask yourself: "Does this belief help me?" For example, you might decide that a certain belief is not helping you when it leads you to feel blue (e.g., feel depressed), to do things that are unhelpful to you (e.g., isolating yourself), or to physically feel worse (e.g., to feel more tired).
(b) You may ask yourself, "There is any evidence to support my negative belief? Is it logical?" For example, you might think "I can't stand feeling so tired and depressed." But if you stop a moment and really think about this you will observe you can stand it: you are waking up every morning, you are reading this material, etc. So even though it may be difficult to cope, you can stand it.

Use the D box to write what you said to yourself to debate and dispute your negative thoughts.

*Alternative thoughts-**E – Effective/Helpful Beliefs***

Once you have successfully debated against your negative beliefs, you need to change them with alternative and more effective or more helpful beliefs.

The healthier alternatives are:

- ***Preferences*** – are thoughts that express the fact that you wish something very badly, but accept that it may not happened the way you wanted. For example, you might think, "I really wish I can concentrate better," instead of saying, "I MUST be focused and 100% concentrated."
- ***Anti-Awfulizing*** – are thoughts that express the fact that a situation is very bad, without thinking it is 100% a catastrophe. For example, you might think, "Not having energy to finish my work is really bad, but I will try to finish it tomorrow," instead of thinking "Not finishing my work is AWFUL!"
- ***High Frustration Tolerance*** – are thoughts that express the fact that even though you may find a situation very difficult to cope with, you can stand it. For example, you might think, "I hate not being able to sleep, but I'll just keep finding new ways to solve this problem" instead of thinking "I can't stand insomnia, it's absolutely unbearable!"
- ***Contextual evaluations*** *regarding:*
  (a) the self- ➔ anti-self-downing – are thoughts that express the fact that you can accept and appreciate yourself, even when you're not perfect or make mistake. So for example, you might think, "I am not that confident as I used to be, but that it is ok, I'm still a good, worthwhile person which can have some weaknesses" instead of thinking, "I'm a worthless and weak person."
  (b) the others ➔ anti-other-downing – are thoughts that express the fact that you can accept others, regardless of the flaws they have or the mistakes they might have made. For example, you might think, "I'm sad that my sister it's

not visiting me more often, but she is a caring and loving sister trying to help me anytime I need" instead of thinking, "She is a bad sister because she visits me rarely."

(c) the life- anti-life-downing – are thoughts that express the fact you accept your life the way it is, even when it is not exactly as you would like it to be. For example, you might think, "My life it is not as I expected to be, but beside the bad things there are also some things which brighten my days," instead of thinking "My life is ended now that I have depression, nothing will ever be the same."

The new effect-**F's** – **More Healthier Emotions and Behaviors**.

Now, you will start to experience the results of all your hard work. This new way of thinking will help you to: (1) feel better emotionally, for example, you may feel less strong negative emotions (e.g., sad but not depressed, regretful but not guilty) and more positive (calmer, happier), (2) act in a more helpful way, for example, you want to go out with your friends or do exercises, and (3) feel better physically, for example, you might feel more energetic and less tensed.

2.4.6 Managing Depression with Emotive Techniques

Emotive techniques will help you challenge and change your negative thoughts. There are several strategies that you can use: (1) humorous methods which you can use to challenge your thoughts and make fun of them, (2) songs, poems, metaphors or other experiential exercises and (3) shame-attacking exercises in which you have to deliberately act in a shameful way in public in order to learn to accept you unconditionally and to tolerate the associated discomfort. Before choosing an exercise, you should have discussed it with your therapist. Keep in mind that the exercise should challenge you to break a minor social norm which does not have a major impact on your life, like wearing different shoes, singing on the street etc.

2.4.7 Be Your Own Therapist

Don't forget!

1. Not always we can change the negative situations in our life, but we can change our thoughts, and this can make us feel better.
2. A lot of exercise is needed in order to change your thinking style, it's like driving a car, it needs a lot of practice so that it becomes a habit.

These techniques will help you to manage your depression symptoms. You can use them in any situation in the future when you may feel overwhelmed and/or distressed.

References

Beck, A. T., Rush, A. J., Shaw, B. F., & Emery, G. (1979). *Cognitive therapy of depression*. New York: Guilford Press.

Beck, J. S. (1995). *Cognitive therapy: Basics and beyond*. New York: Guilford Press.

Boland, R., & Keller, M. (2009). Course and outcome of depression. In I. Gotlib & C. Hammen (Eds.), *Handbook of depression* (pp. 23–44). New York: Guilford Press.

David, D., Szentagotai, A., Lupu, V., & Cosman, D. (2008). Rational emotive behavior therapy, cognitive therapy, and medication in the treatment of major depressive disorder: A randomized clinical trial, posttreatment outcomes, and six-month follow-up. *Journal of Clinical Psychology, 64*(6), 728–746. https://doi.org/10.1002/jclp.20487

DeRubeis, R. J., Hollon, S. D., Amsterdam, J. D., Shelton, R. C., Young, P. R., Salomon, R. M., … Gallop, R. (2005). Cognitive therapy vs medications in the treatment of moderate to severe depression. *Archives of General Psychiatry, 62*(4), 409–416. https://doi.org/10.1001/archpsyc.62.4.409

DiGiuseppe, R. A., Doyle, K. A., Dryden, W., & Backx, W. (2014). *A practitioner's guide to rational-emotive behavior therapy*. New York: Oxford University Press.

Dobson, D., & Dobson, K. S. (2009). *Evidenced-based practice of cognitive-behavioral therapy*. New York: Guilford Press.

Dryden, W. (2006). *Counselling in a nutshell*. London: Sage.

Dryden, W. (2009). *Skills in rational emotive behaviour counselling & psychotherapy*. London: Sage.

Dryden, W., & Branch, R. (2008). *Fundamentals of rational emotive behaviour therapy: A training handbook*. Chichester: Wiley.

Ellis, A. (2002). *Overcoming resistance: A rational emotive behavior therapy integrated approach*. New York: Springer.

Ellis, A., & Grieger, R. M. (1977). *Handbook of rational-emotive therapy*. New York: Springer.

First, M. B., Spitzer, R. L., Gibbon, M., & Williams, J. B. W. (1996). *Structured clinical interview for DSM-IV axis I disorders, clinician version (SCID-CV)*. Washington, DC: American Psychiatric Press.

Garland, A., & Scott, J. (2005). Depression. In N. Kazantsis, F. P. Deane, K. R. Ronan, & L. L'Abate (Eds.), *Using homework assignments in cognitive behaviour therapy* (pp. 196–215). New York: Routledge.

Hamilton, M. (1967). Development of a rating scale for primary depressive illness. *Journal of Social and Clinical Psychology, 6*, 278–296. https://doi.org/10.1111/j.2044-8260.1967.tb00530.x

Lambert, M. J., & Barley, D. E. (2002). Research summary on the therapeutic relationship and psychotherapy. In J. C. Norcross (Ed.), *Psychotherapy relationships that work: Therapist contributions and responsiveness to patients* (pp. 17–36). New York: Oxford University Press.

Rogers, C. R. (1957). The necessary and sufficient conditions of therapeutic personality change. *Journal of Consulting Psychology, 21*(2), 95–103. https://doi.org/10.1037/h0045357

Szentagotai, A., David, D., Lupu, V., & Cosman, D. (2008). Rational emotive behavior therapy versus cognitive therapy versus pharmacotherapy in the treatment of major depressive disorder: Mechanisms of change analysis. *Psychotherapy: Theory, Research, Practice, Training, 45*(4), 523–538. https://doi.org/10.1037/a0014332

Walen, S. R., DiGiuseppe, R., & Dryden, W. (1992). *A practitioner's guide to rational emotive therapy* (2nd ed.). New York: Oxford University Press.

Chapter 3
Rational-Emotive and Cognitive-Behavior Therapy for Major Depressive Disorder in Children and Adolescents

3.1 Description of a Group REBT Intervention for MDD in Children and Adolescents – A Therapist Guide

In this chapter, we will introduce the principles and structure of a group-delivered REBT treatment protocol designed for depressed children and adolescents. The protocol was already tested in a clinical trial, comparing group REBT, medication (i.e., sertraline), and their combination in treating youth depression by considering multiple levels of analysis (i.e., cognitive, subjective, and biological – serum serotonin and norepinephrine), and the results have already been published (Iftene, Predescu, Stefan, & David, 2015).

3.1.1 Treatment Goals

Following the principles of REBT, the protocol combined cognitive restructuring techniques with behavior activation and problem-solving techniques in order to change irrational beliefs (i.e., demandingness and self-downing, as main irrational beliefs triggering depression, but also awfulizing and low frustration tolerance) into rational ones (i.e., preference/flexibility and unconditional self-acceptance), and develop healthy behavior patterns. The major treatment goals can be formulated as follows:

(a) restructuring demandingness in particular, which is considered a core belief in major depressive disorder (e.g., Ellis, 1987; Solomon, Arnow, Gotlib, & Wind, 2003);
(b) encouraging unconditional self-acceptance and other rational beliefs;

D. Cândea et al., *REBT in the Treatment of Subclinical and Clinical Depression*, SpringerBriefs in Psychology, https://doi.org/10.1007/978-3-030-03968-4_3

(c) targeting secondary problems like depression about depression (meta-emotions);
(d) encouraging an active lifestyle, developing social abilities and problem-solving strategies.

3.1.2 Session by Session Structure

The protocol was delivered in 16 weekly group sessions, the first 14 for intervention and 2 for progress consolidation. Each session lasted 60–90 min. Regarding session structure, we followed the recommendation suggested by CBT in general (Beck et al., 1979; Beck, 1995), group CBT (Bieling, McCabe, & Antony, 2004), and group CBT adaptations for adolescents (Clarke, Lewinsohn, Hops, & Seeley, 1990), tested in previous trials (e.g., Clarke et al., 1999; Clarke et al., 2001), and respected a similar session-structure throughout the treatment progress.

3.1.2.1 Session 1 – Group Forming and Cohesion

Given the fact that the first sessions are very important in setting expectancies, building adherence motivation, and preventing drop-out, we will describe them in more detail. Generally, the first session should cover four major goals: (1) group forming, (2) building therapeutic relationship, (3) psychoeducation, and (4) setting treatment expectancies for each patient. Except for these specific content elements of the first session, the rest of components will be tackled in the following sessions too. The structure of the first sessions comprises the following:

Agenda setting (and offering a motivation for this) – it is important to state the importance of agenda setting right from the beginning of treatment, so participants would know what to expect in the future – in this session, we would tell participants that we will proceed by knowing each other, discussing their mood and diagnosed problems, then discussing about CBT/REBT and their expectancies, providing information about depression, choosing a homework assignment and providing a summary.

Group forming and building cohesion – in group therapy, cohesion is considered the equivalent of therapeutic relationship in individual psychotherapy, and it is one of its evidence-based components (Norcross, 2002). In order to help each other in the treatment process, participants first need to trust each other – therefore, it is important to establish preliminary ground rules regarding confidentiality. In this sense, the therapists discuss with the group participants that all information they share is confidential, with some very important exceptions, namely situations when the adolescent is considered to endanger herself or others. Also, participants are encouraged to keep all shared information to themselves, but, since we cannot exert a real control in this respect, it is important to give the adolescents the option of withholding private information

(Clarke et al., 1990). Regarding the therapeutic relationship, we used the general principles of empathy, unconditional self-acceptance and congruence, and we followed the recommendations of Clarke et al. (1990) in terms of building a rapport based on collaboration, with the therapist displaying a friendly, understanding, yet firm approach towards the adolescents, encouraging them as much as possible in sharing opinions and suggestions. While adolescents feel more comfortable when treated as adults, trying, as a therapist, to behave in a way similar to adolescents (e.g., try to be "cool") is generally discouraged, because it blurs the boundaries of the therapeutic relationship and undermines the therapists' authority, which is necessary when dealing with potential disruptive behaviors.

In order to increase the level of cohesiveness, therapists are advised to introduce icebreakers in the beginning of the first sessions, organize between-session breaks, and constantly build connections among the participants' shared experiences (e.g., "It seems like both X and Y are facing a similar problem").

Mood Assessment – In the beginning of the first session, participants are asked to assess their mood, by indicating how happy, sad, depressed, angry, etc. they are by expressing this verbally and also by using brief instruments, adapted for adolescents, such as the example below, adapted from the PsyPills application (David & David, **2013**) in Fig. 3.1. Also, we recommend using validated assess-

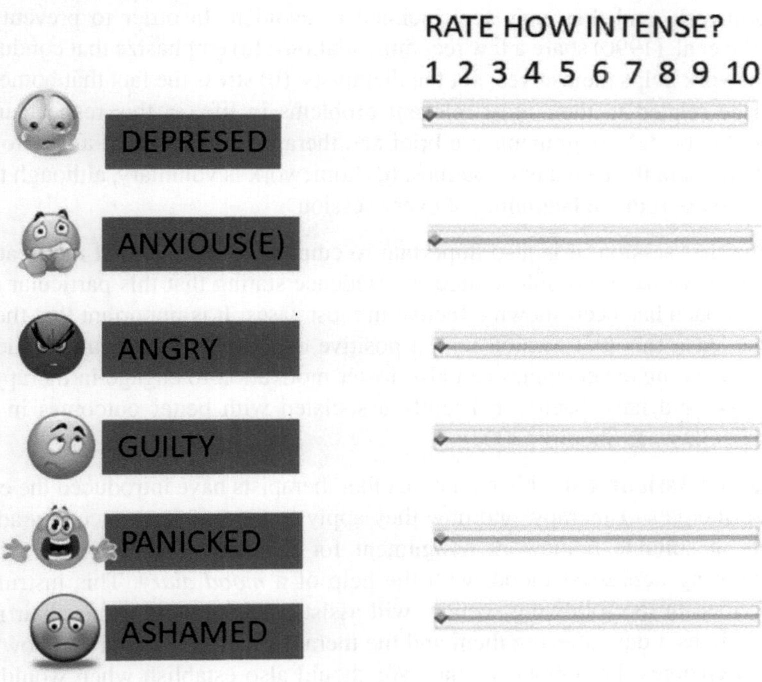

Fig. 3.1 Mood rating form. (PsyPills, David & David, 2013)

ment instruments for depression (e.g., the CDI), since they constitute an objective measure of treatment progress. By having an objective measure of symptoms, we can track the progress adolescents make in therapy and we can offer them a useful feedback in this sense (also in a graphical form).

Psychoeducation – The purpose of psychoeducation in this first session is threefold:

1. We provide a brief description of their condition in terms of the REBT/CBT model. That is, we explain that depression is a negative, dysfunctional (i.e., not helpful) emotion triggered by irrational, rigid thinking, which further leads to isolation tendencies and apathy. Engaging in fewer activities, we prevent positive events from happening, which further maintains our depressed feelings.
2. We provide a brief description of the REBT theory (i.e., the ABC model) and how we can address depression by using REBT/CBT techniques (e.g., cognitive restructuring, behavioral activation).
3. We normalize expectations about treatment and its success. At this point, it is important to emphasize that applying the REBT/CBT techniques requires sustained effort on patients' behalf, because cognitive and behavioral changes are not easy to implement and cannot be achieved without further practice. While we would also explain this when dealing with adults in a therapy group, we have to be more cautious with adolescents when discussing homework, since it is likely that some of them will assimilate the word and the concept of *homework* to schoolwork, and they may feel inclined to avoid it. In order to prevent this, Clarke et al. (1990) share a few recommendations: (a) emphasize that conducting homework helps themselves, not the therapists; (b) stress the fact that homework will be related to their most relevant problems in life, in this respect, unlike schoolwork; (c) assignments are brief and therapists have to find a way to integrate them in the teenagers' routines; (d) homework is voluntary, although therapists assess it in the beginning of every session.

In the first session, it is also important to emphasize the fact that the treatment works, that we have multiple sources of evidence stating that this particular treatment approach has been shown effective in most cases. It is important that the participants leave this first session with a positive expectancy for treatment success. Positive outcome expectancies can also foster motivation to engage in therapy and homework, and have been consistently associated with better outcomes in CBT (Arnkoff, Glass, & Shapiro, 2002).

Homework Assignment – Given the fact that therapists have introduced the essential principles of therapy, and how they apply to the problems faced by adolescents, a suitable homework assignment for the first session would refer to monitoring depressed mood, with the help of a *mood diary*. This instrument, described in the following section, will assist adolescents in rating their mood three times a day, offering them and the therapist a clearer picture of how their mood changes throughout the day. We should also establish when would be a right time for the adolescents to do their homework; in this way, they can choose the right time-frame for them and feel more in control.

Summarizing – At the end of the first session, a summary should be provided in order to offer some structure and provide key messages to the adolescents. The summary should focus on the most important parts in every section discussed so far (i.e., getting to know each other, mood assessment, what is depression and how we can treat it, the importance of homework).

Soliciting Feedback – Finally, therapists should elicit feedback from the adolescents in terms of what they understood, whether they liked participating in the session, and whether they think this therapy can help them.

3.1.2.2 Session 2 – Problem Lists

The general structure of session 2 resembles the general structure of REBT/CBT interventions. As some components have already been discussed, we will present in more detail only those components which have not yet been introduced.

Agenda setting – the objectives of the second session should be highlighted, namely assessing mood, reviewing homework, further consolidating the group and establishing a list of problems for each participant.

Mood assessment: participants are asked to offer brief statements on their mood and complete a mood evaluation form.

Homework review: when assessing homework, it is important to build connections among group members by discussing similarities. Therapists can start from one example of mood diary and ask the other participants if theirs is similar and, if not, in what way it is dissimilar. In this way, homework assessment becomes a dynamic process, also encouraging group cohesion (Bieling et al., 2004). It is also very important to discuss eventual difficulties with homework. This principle in homework assessment should be followed in the forthcoming sessions too.

Bridging from the previous session: in this part therapists should connect what was discussed in the previous session to the objectives of session 2. In this case, the therapists can say that depression (with its causes and effects, explained in session 1), although a shared emotional experience among the group members, looks differently in each individual; therefore, participants should formulate their own problems/goals in terms of mood and behavior change.

Formulating a problem list for each participant. In session 2, starting from their goals, participants will formulate individualized problem lists. In order to provide some structure, problems would be grouped into emotional (e.g., feeling sad and depressed), behavioral (e.g., low grades), or social/communication problems (e.g., arguing with parents). Therapists should assist adolescents with formulating their problems in these terms and also in ensuring that they have covered the most important issues. Like when reviewing homework, listing problems should be a dynamic process, all adolescents participating in the conversation and connecting their experiences. For instance, starting from one example, we can involve another participant (e.g., "Maria said she feels especially sad in the morning, thinking a difficult day follows. Is this the case for you also, George?"). When ending this activity, each participant should have an individualized problem list, usually comprising 6–8 problems. It is also worth mentioning to the participants that in a group session, we cannot focus on each problem on each participant's list, but we would use strategies which have been shown to be generally effective (i.e., applied on specific examples provided by them), and the participants will use them with reference to their particular concerns.

Session 2, like the previous one, should end with **homework assignment, summarizing, and soliciting feedback.**

3.1.2.3 Sessions 3 and 4 – Behavior Activation

Sessions 3 and 4 should be focused on behavior activation, and address three major goals:

1. conceptualizing the link between engaging in pleasant behaviors and mood;
2. identifying potentially pleasant activities, and
3. activity planning and monitoring.

Starting from the conceptualization of depression introduced in session 1, therapists can present the concepts of downward and upward spiral (Clarke et al., 1990, Fig. 3.2), emphasizing the idea that not engaging in pleasant and social activities leads to depressed mood, which further prevents people from engaging in such activities (because when feeling depressed, it doesn't feel like doing much and they keep planning to do activities when they feel better, which will not happen soon). Therefore, it is important to engage in pleasant activities even if it doesn't feel like it because, in time, this will enhance positive mood. In order to facilitate understanding, therapists can use a graphical representation, like the one presented in Fig. 3.2. Next, pleasant activities would be identified for each participant, choosing from a list (and completing it if necessary). Again, we should turn this activity into an interactive one, engaging all participants in discussing and choosing pleasant activities. At this point, therapists should be careful to choose activities which are naturally reinforced (e.g., pleasant) and easy to accomplish; performing them will enhance positive mood and foster self-efficacy altogether. Also, we should identify and address possible obstacles (e.g., feeling too tired, bad weather), so adolescents will have several solutions in case they emerge. Choosing pleasant activities, discussing their advantages and obstacles, along with introducing activity monitoring and planning should generally be comprised in session 3, while in session 4, therapists and participants would discuss how these principles work in practice and what can be done to improve daily and weekly schedules.

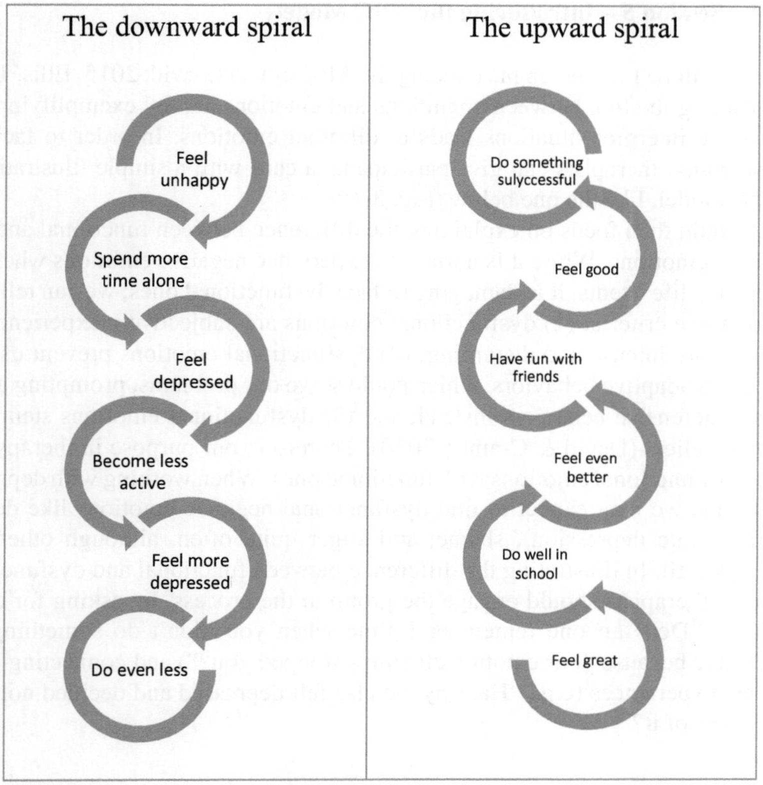

Fig. 3.2 The downward and upward spiral of negative mood. (Adapted after Clarke et al., 1990)

Activity planning and monitoring, introduced in session 3, will continue throughout the therapeutic process, since they are considered cornerstones in the intervention. Also, as therapy progresses, we should be able to include more complex activities in the participants' repertoire (e.g., taking a walk would be a suitable activity for session 2, while by mid-treatment we would encourage more complex activities, like inviting some friends over). In combination with mood monitoring (also continuously done), activity monitoring will provide valuable information for therapists and patients alike; for instance, the link between behaviors and mood will be more explicitly portrayed, thus reinforcing our theoretical accounts on the CBT/REBT model of depression; adolescents would become more motivated once they see the connection between engaging in pleasant activities and mood, and increased self-efficacy (resulting from performing behavioral tasks) will also be a source for positive mood. For activity monitoring and planning, we can use forms like the ones presented in Appendices 2 and 3.

3.1.2.4 Session 5 – Introducing the ABC Model

Session 5 will be focused on introducing the ABC model (David, 2015; Ellis, 1994), by explaining the link between cognitions and emotions and by exemplifying how the way we interpret situations leads to different emotions. In order to facilitate understanding, therapists can give participants a card with a simple illustration of the ABC model, like the one below (Fig. 3.3):

We should then focus on explaining the difference between functional and dysfunctional emotions. While it is normal to experience negative emotions when facing negative life events, it is damaging to face dysfunctional ones; we can tell them apart on three criteria: (1) dysfunctional emotions are subjectively experienced as such, as more intense and disturbing; (2) dysfunctional emotions prevent us from engaging in adaptive behaviors, which could solve our problems, prompting avoidance and defensive behaviors instead, and (3) dysfunctional emotions stem from irrational beliefs (David & Cramer, 2010). Therefore, our purpose in therapy is to replace dysfunctional emotions with functional ones. When working with depressed adolescents, we may expect to find dysfunctional negative emotions like depression (i.e., state depression), shame, and anger quite often, although others can emerge as well. In illustrating the difference between functional and dysfunctional emotions, therapists should engage the group in the process, by asking for examples (e.g., "Does anyone remember a time when you didn't do something you should have because your emotions/feelings stopped you?") and connecting group members experiences (e.g., "Has anyone else felt depressed and decided not to go out because of it?").

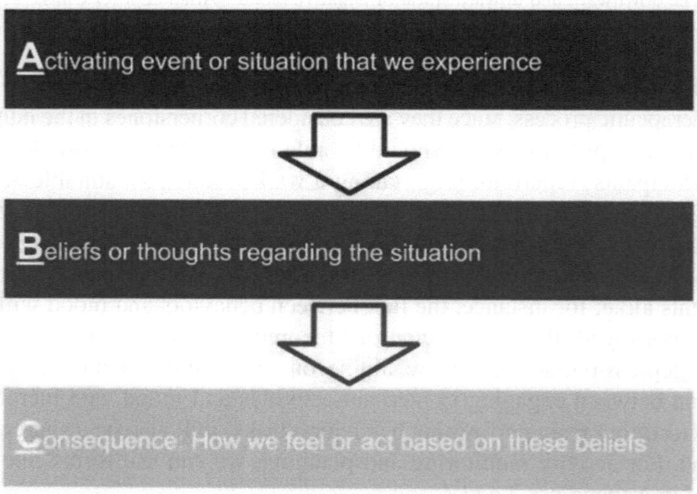

Fig. 3.3 The ABC model – functional and dysfunctional emotions

A brief exercise, asking participants to rate their current mood would be useful at this point for exemplifying the distinction between functional and dysfunctional emotions. Importantly, adolescents will be encouraged from now on to explicitly use the distinction between functional and dysfunctional emotions in their daily mood monitoring; thus we would see how emotions shift from dysfunctional to functional as therapy progresses. For a graphic representation of the distinction, we can use the following illustrations (Fig. 3.4):

We would then restate the idea that emotions, functional and dysfunctional, result from the beliefs that we hold in relation to different events. Rational beliefs lead to functional emotions and irrational beliefs lead to dysfunctional ones; we would not recommend further explaining at this point, since all types of irrational beliefs will be discussed in future sessions; but we would rather introduce the concept of a psychological pill. The concept of psychological pills © was introduced by David (2006), and it refers to a set of phrases comprising rational beliefs, generally found to be effective in dealing with particular dysfunctional emotions (e.g., depression, anxiety), given to participants in the form of coping cards. We would discuss one example with our group, for instance, one related to depression as the one presented in Box 3.1.

Box 3.1 Psychological pill © for depression (After David, 2007)

"I wish the situation were different, but I know that my wish does not become reality just because I want it"

"I can accept that things I don't want happen in life, although it is disappointing"

"What I did was wrong, but I always remain a valuable person, because I am human"

"Maybe the way I reacted is a sign of weakness, but it does not show my value as a person"

"Even if I don't always do as well as I want to, I am still a kind and valuable person"

"I am happy with myself, although I know I'm not perfect"

In discussing the psychological pill above, we should approach each phrase, explaining its meaning and how it applies to the participants' life. It is very likely that some participants will benefit from one or two phrases more than from the others, and it is our aim to identify the relevant phrases for each individual. At first, participants are instructed to review the pill every morning, along with their mood and activity monitoring in order to practice it before using it in more distressing circumstances. Eventually, their purpose will be this: to provide comfort, relatively rapidly, in future difficult situations.

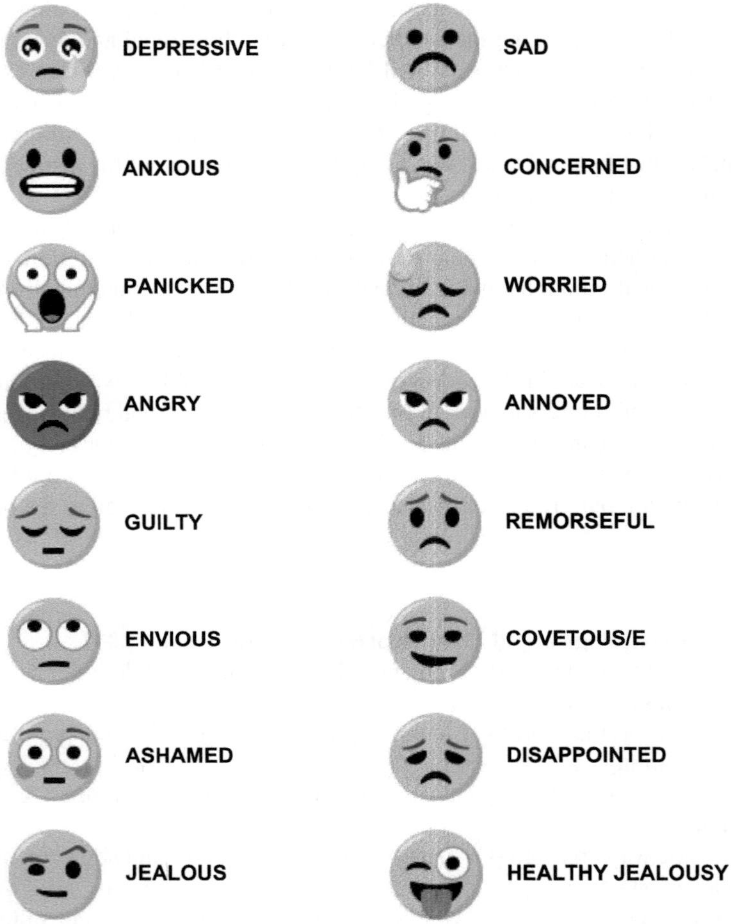

Fig. 3.4 Dysfunctional and functional emotions. (Adapted from The "PsyPills" app, David & David, 2013)

Also, when conducting REBT in groups, participants are encouraged to give each other feedback and support in restructuring irrational beliefs and replacing them with rational ones. As some participants are expected to understand and endorse rational thinking at a faster pace than others, they can become a model and an important source of encouragement for the others (Ellis & Dryden, 1997). This is why, when restructuring irrational beliefs, therapists are encouraged to rely on the group and explicitly ask members for suggestions (e.g., "How could we rephrase this belief in a rational manner? Does anyone have any thoughts on this?").

3.1.2.5 Session 6 – Focusing on Demandingness

In session 6, therapists will begin approaching the central irrational belief – demandingness (DEM). We would begin with demandingness because it is considered a core belief in major depressive disorder (Ellis, 1987; Solomon et al., 2003), all other evaluative beliefs (i.e., self and other downing, awfulizing, low frustration tolerance) deriving from it. Like previously stated (chapter), DEM refers to formulating one's desires and goals in absolutistic, inflexible terms, thus making the individual vulnerable when facing negative life events which are connected to one's purposes (e.g., "I must succeed and I cannot accept it if it doesn't happen"). Everybody has absolutistic demands; it depends how many, to which fields they apply, and how rigid they are when challenged. The more absolutistic demands we have, the more it is likely to face dysfunctional emotions because they will be triggered in numerous situations. It is therefore recommended to identify our demands and gradually replace them with preferences – rational beliefs expressing goals and desires in a flexible, realistic manner (e.g., "I want to succeed, and I do all the best in my power to do that, but I accept that things don't always work the way I want them to"). It is important at this point to stress the idea that more DEM does not equal more determination and ambition, but it represents an irrational formulation of goals, since, in reality, literally nothing must happen one way or another. On the other hand, holding a rational belief about a purpose expresses both determination (e.g., "I will do the best I can") and the acceptance of reality. Also, it is important to stress the differences between DEM and preference in terms of behavioral outcomes too; while DEM (i.e., when triggered in negative situations) leads to dysfunctional emotions, and consequently, to dysfunctional behaviors (e.g., avoidance, withdrawal), holding a rational belief in negative situations leads to functional negative emotions, and, eventually, to problem solving attempts (or peace of mind, when nothing can be done).

We recommend the use of both explanations and metaphors in order to transmit this idea. A possibly useful exercise would imply the reformulation of the participants' purposes and desires in a rational manner, and discuss what the consequences would be if a relevant negative event occurred (e.g., holding a rational belief about school success and obtaining a bad grade). In order to replace irrational beliefs with rational ones, it might be necessary to challenge/dispute them. In order to do that, we can use various techniques, the most common being:

(a) Logical disputation – "Is it logical to think that because you wish for something, than that thing must absolutely happen?"
(b) Empirical disputation – "If you say things <u>mustn't</u> happen this way, how come they still happen?"
(c) Pragmatic disputation – "Does it serve you to think this way?"

After this session, therapists are recommended to assign a homework exercise consisting of identifying and challenging two demands they notice the following week. When assigning this homework, we also provide written examples of disputation, so to make it easier for participants to replace their beliefs.

3.1.2.6 Sessions 7 and 8 – Focusing on Global Evaluation and Promoting Unconditional Acceptance

Another important irrational belief particularly related to depression is self-downing or self-depreciation (Ellis, 1994; Knaus, 2012). Basically, holding this irrational belief when facing negative events (like failures) translates into global, negative evaluations of self-worth (e.g., "I am incapable, worthless), which further lead to dysfunctional feelings of depression, shame and guilt (like those characteristic of the clinical presentation of major depressive disorder). What happens is that, starting from a particular event, the individual makes a faulty generalization of oneself and concludes he/she is incapable or worthless overall, as a person (e.g., Ellis & Dryden, 1997). When applied to other individuals, this distortion is called other-downing and when referring to life in general we talk about life-downing/life-depreciation. The rational counterpart of self-depreciation is unconditional self-acceptance (USA), which refers to fully accepting oneself as a human being, without rating oneself in terms of performances (Ellis, 2013). In this sense, unconditional acceptance involves not rating one's worth in any way (either good or bad), because humans are too complex to be accurately rated; on the other hand, behaviors can and should be rated. Promoting an acceptance-based attitude towards the self and others, USA is promoted in many forms of therapy, leading to positive emotional and behavioral consequences (Bernard, 2013).

Since it is a highly relevant irrational belief in the context of depression (Ellis, 1994; Knaus, 2012), the protocol includes two sessions to cover unconditional self-acceptance, one for explaining the concept and the other for practice and reinstatement. A useful way to start discussing the distinction between global evaluation and acceptance would be to ask participants to provide examples of them both, instances when they felt defeated, lost, depressed after they lost or failed at something, and instances when they kept their spirits high even if loosing or not succeeding felt bad. We can stress the idea that accepting oneself is also different from accepting one's behaviors and believing we are perfect; on the contrary, we are more open to criticism and improvement if we lose the burden of proving our worth as individuals. In terms of consequences, we can illustrate the difference between the two by using stories, movies, metaphors, or pictures, like the one below (Fig. 3.5):

We can also include exercises like listing one's strengths and weaknesses and then join them into a "personality profile", which is unlikely to change in the face of failures or successes.

Fig. 3.5 Accepting myself versus self-downing. (Adapted from Bernard, Vernon, Terjesen, & Kurasaki, 2013)

3.1.2.7 Session 9 – Focusing on Low Frustration Tolerance

Since it is very likely for adolescents to experience anger related problems, it is important to target one of its most important sources, low frustration tolerance (LFT) and replace it with high frustration tolerance. In this sense, data have shown that LFT is particularly related to depression in adolescents (Marcotte, 1996), so targeting it is especially important. LFT is usually expressed with thoughts like "I can't stand this", "This is unbearable", "I can't tolerate this", and, in the face of negative life events, it leads to anger. First, therapists identify situations when group members have experienced such thoughts, and then assess the emotions they reported. Then, therapists explain how believing a situation is unbearable is wrong, since many situations considered like this have actually been endured quite often (e.g., arguing, liking someone who doesn't like you back, being bullied, waiting in a queue etc). The rational alternative would be thinking of the trigger situation in terms of unpleasantness, but not in terms of it being unbearable. After explaining the distinction, therapists can form rational statements starting from the participants' examples (e.g., "I dislike not being respected by my colleagues, but I can stand it"), and then, assign as homework an exercise involving exposure to annoying situations (e.g., stand in a queue, doing a disliked schoolwork exercise) while practicing the rational thoughts.

3.1.2.8 Session 10 – Focusing on Awfulizing/Catastrophizing

Another important irrational belief is awfulizing/catastrophizing, namely interpreting negative events in a catastrophic manner, like the worst possible outcome has occurred. However, while negative events are by definition, bad and unpleasant, catastrophes are rare; therefore, it is adaptive to conceptualize negative events as bad, and not catastrophic, because the negative associated emotions will also be different; interpreting an event as bad will lead to functional emotions such as sadness and concern, while awfulizing will lead to dysfunctional emotions, like depression and anxiety. After explaining this distinction, it would be useful to apply various techniques in order to restructure awfulizing and replace it with badness, and teach group members to do the same. One useful technique is the "catastrophe scale ": first, the client is asked to name an event which he/she considered awful (rated with 8, 9, or 10 on a 1 to 10 scale of catastrophes), and then think of the most dramatic events which could potentially happen, and rate them with 8, 9, or 10. After this, the participant is asked to rerate the initial events he/she mentioned. What usually happens is that people see that what they rate as catastrophic is, in reality, bad, but manageable.

3.1.2.9 Session 11 – Focusing on Secondary/Meta-Emotions

Secondary emotions, or meta-emotions (i.e., emotions triggered when the activating event is also an emotional state) are essential targets in psychotherapy, sometimes leading to strong and debilitating emotional consequences (e.g., depression about depression, anxiety about anxiety). Particularly in the case of depression, secondary emotions can further extent the vicious circle of depressive mood, and they are a primary focus of intervention. For instance, once feeling depressed, the patient may have irrational beliefs about being depressed (e.g., "I shouldn't be depressed, I am a loser for being depressed"), and thus a secondary emotion (i.e., secondary, or meta- depression) emerges. In order to efficiently address them both, REBT recommends starting with the meta-emotion (Dryden & DiGiuseppe, 1990). In the group session, participants are learned to recognize their secondary emotions and deal with them before targeting primary emotions. To find out whether there is a secondary emotion following the primary one, the therapists can ask the question: "Besides depression, did you feel anything else in relation to your depression?"

3.1.2.10 Session 12 – Relaxation

In this protocol, we decided to teach adolescents the Jacobson relaxation technique (Jacobson, 1929); this technique achieves a state of relaxation by taking a more active stance (i.e., alternatively tensing and relaxing the major muscle groups for 10 s) and thus seems more suitable for adolescents. Also, it is relatively easy to learn and provides an early experience of success and self-efficacy, encouraging adolescents to practice it further on (Rohde, 2011). At first, therapists should offer a rationale for the technique – relaxation can ease stress and anxiety, and also can help with sleeping problems. Then, the therapists practice it with the group and solicit feedback related to how the participants managed to use the technique, how relaxed they managed to be and how their emotions changes during the process. Afterwards, conducting a relaxation exercise for 10 min should be assigned as a homework, and the progress and potential difficulties should be addressed in the following sessions. For instance, some adolescents may report the fact that they do not manage to relax with the exercise and consider abandoning its practice. In this case, therapists should mention that such difficulties are common initially and that they should try to practice the technique a few times before they decide it is useful or not (Rohde, 2011).

3.1.2.11 Sessions 13 and 14 – Problem Solving and Social Skills

We know that depression is associated with poor social functioning in adolescents, with depressive symptoms predicting longitudinally social problems and the other way around (Verboom, Sijtsema, Verhulst, Penninx, & Ormel, 2014). That is, poor social functioning may lead to and maintain depressive symptoms, and depressive symptoms further lead to low social functioning, probably due to depressive mood and social isolation. This is why building social skills, negotiation, and problem solving abilities is an important goal in therapy. In the group sessions, therapists introduce communication and problem solving skills, then conduct exercises and quizzes, practice role-playing, and assign homework. Regarding the specific skills we worked on, we followed the suggestions indicated in the protocol devised by Clarke et al. (1990). For instance, we focused on stating positive feelings, appropriate self-disclosure, and stating negative feelings in an assertive manner. After introducing the concepts, therapists and group participants tried to "solve" together exercises comprising these skills, in an interactive way (e.g., "You are upset that your friend did not congratulate you on your birthday. Should you express your annoyance with that or let it go? When should you express it, now or at a later time? How should you phrase it?"). In the example above, adolescents would be encouraged to express their discontent in an assertive manner, express it as soon as possible, and phrase it in a way which emphasizes their own feelings, and the friend's behavior, and not the other person as a whole (e.g., "I felt sad when you didn't say Happy Birthday to me", and not "You are not a true friend" or "You clearly don't care about me"). In order to see the difference, participants can role-play more alternatives (with one of them acting as herself and another as the friend) and experience how it is more likely for the other to react to different statements.

With reference to problem solving, we followed the approach proposed by D'Zurilla and Nezu (1999) and Eskin (2012). In this view, effective problem solving implies several steps, which are discussed and practiced in therapy:

(a) **Setting a positive orientation** towards problems as opposed to a negative one. A positive orientation involves seeing problems more like challenges than like threats, believing that problems have solutions, self-efficacy, believing that solving problems takes effort and time, and engaging in problem solving. In opposition, a negative orientation involves seeing problems as threats, becoming easily frustrated when dealing with a problem, and low self-efficacy. In order to change this, therapists use psychoeducation, cognitive restructuring techniques, behavior experiments (e.g., solving a smaller matter, like finding out information about future college prospects).
(b) **Defining the problem** in order to make it an observable, measurable goal. From a list of potential problems, participants choose their problems and define them in terms of who is involved, where it happens, when it is salient, what makes it a problem, and how it unfolds. Answering these questions is already an important step for putting the matter into a more concrete and constructive perspective.
(c) **Brainstorming** – participants think of solutions, as many as possible, without being critical at this point. In group, they are encouraged to think of solutions for the others' problems as well.
(d) **Choose a solution and make a plan**. At this point, group members critically analyze all options and list advantages and disadvantages for all the potential solutions. In order to do that, therapists can provide some guiding questions, such as: is this solution compatible with my short and long term goals? How long would it take to implement it? How will it affect me and the others? Is it feasible/doable?
(e) **Implementing the solution and assessing its effectiveness**. Now, participants should analyze whether the solution was successfully implemented, and if not, what obstacles emerged. In case it was implemented but it wasn't effective, then another solution from the list may be a better option. Moreover, we have to consider the fact that even if a solution is suitable and feasible, there may be many relapses along the way, and in case these occur, participants are instructed to use cognitive restructuring techniques to overcome self-defeating thoughts which may emerge.

3.1.2.12 Sessions 15 and 16 – Relapse Prevention and Consolidating Progress

The last sessions will refer to maintaining treatment gains and relapse prevention. Following previous guidelines (Clarke et al., 1990), we introduced (1) maintaining gains, (2) emergency/prevention planning, and (3) early recognition as treatment goals. For maintaining gains, therapists reviewed the ABC models (cognitive and behavioral), activity plans, problem solving and communication strategies sheets, and discussed their personalized psychological pills. Also, group members discussed their short and long term future plans, envisioned potential obstacles, and listed possible solutions, referring to both action plans and emotional coping.

In order to prevent relapse, it is important to plan ahead. Since it is more likely that future depressive episodes may occur following negative or challenging life events (e.g., a breakup, the loss of a loved one, moving to another place), it is useful to prepare and list some cognitive and behavioral strategies which could be applied when/whether such events happen. Surely, some events are predictable and very likely (e.g., graduating high-school), while others are unpredictable but likely (e.g., getting married), or unpredictable and less likely (e.g., being in a serious car crash). Group members were asked to list such events and discuss coping plans for each category. The plan would usually combine problem solving strategies, with behavioral techniques, and emotional coping strategies (the ABC model, relaxation). For the prevention of full episodes recurrence, it is important for adolescents to recognize depression signs early and take immediate action. Given that cognitive vulnerability has been constantly associated with depression in adolescents (e.g., Hamilton et al., 2014), it is important to acknowledge this and know the signs in advance. While experiencing negative mood is a normal and frequent part of life, it is not to be confounded with depression. In that purpose, adolescents are encouraged to monitor their mood continually, using forms similar to the ones introduced in the first sessions, and, when noticing a more intense, disturbing, or lasting depressive state to use the strategies learned in therapy: plan activities, relaxation techniques, and restructure irrational beliefs by using the ABC model. In case the symptoms persist longer than 2 weeks, adolescents are encouraged to ask for help from psychologists and/or psychiatrists. Overall, the aim of the last two sessions was to help participants become their own psychotherapists, being aware of their cognitive vulnerabilities, recognizing their moods as functional or dysfunctional, and use cognitive and behavioral strategies effectively.

3.2 A Clinical Trial Testing the Protocol for MDD in Children and Adolescents

The protocol previously presented followed the principles of REBT (Dryden & Neenan, 2002; Ellis, 1987), and was developed by adapting the REBT (individual) protocol previously tested with Romanian adults (David et al., 2008), considering guidelines for group CBT in general (Bieling et al., 2004), and group CBT adaptations for adolescents (Clarke et al., 1990). The protocol was administered in 16 group sessions, with 6–8 members in each group. The article comprising the main results was published (Iftene et al., 2015).

Participants (n = 88) were recruited starting 2007, using the following sources: (1) the Clinic of Child and Adolescent Psychiatry and the Psychological Counseling Center in Cluj-Napoca; (2) the Institute for the Advanced Studies of Psychotherapy and Applied Mental Health (Babes-Bolyai University, Cluj-Napoca); (3) the Romanian Association for Cognitive-Behavioral Therapies; (4) the private practice of team members; and (5) press announcements. Participants and their parents signed an informed consent, expressing their agreement to take part in the trial.

In order to enroll in this study, all participants had to be diagnosed with major depressive disorder, following the DSM-IV criteria, and we used the Structured Clinical Interview for DSM-IV as a diagnostic tool (KID-SCID, Hien et al., 1994). The participants were aged 11–17 (m = 15.25, S.D. = 1.91), 49 were females and 39 were males. We used the following exclusion criteria: presence of bipolar disorder, severe conduct disorder, substance use/abuse/dependence, pervasive developmental disorders, psychotic disorders, being actively suicidal or having homicidal ideation, an IQ score lower than 80, concurrent treatment with psychotropic drug (stable stimulant for ADHD permitted) or parallel psychotherapy sessions, two previous failed SSRI trials or a failed trial of CBT for depression, and intolerance to sertraline. After recruitment, they were randomly assigned to one of the three treatment arms.

All intervention forms lasted for 16 weeks, with all the therapy sessions taking place at the same location (the International Institute for the Advanced Studies of Psychotherapy and Applied Mental Health), likewise for the medication sessions and biological measures (the Clinic of Child and Adolescent Psychiatry and the Psychological Counseling Center in Cluj-Napoca). The study had been previously approved by the Romanian National Agency for Medication (No. 7290/24.07.2007).

As previously mentioned, the purpose of this trial was to assess the efficacy of group REBT in comparison to medication and the combination of the two in terms of multiple-level outcomes. Therefore, we focused on (1) symptom/subjective outcomes, measured by the Child Depression Inventory (CDI; Kovacs, 1992), a 27-item instrument designed for children and adolescents, and by the Profile of Mood States, short version, (POMS; Dilorenzo, Bovbjerg, Montgomery, Valdimarsdottir, & Jacobsen, 1999), a widely-used instrument which assesses general distress; (2) cognitive level outcomes, operationalized by the Automatic Thoughts Questionnaire (ATQ; Hollon & Kendall, 1980), designed to assess automatic thoughts particularly related to depression; and (3) biological outcomes – serum serotonin and norepinephrine measured using Cromsystems kits.

The results of the trial indicated the three interventions (group REBT/CBT, medication, and their combination) to be similarly effective on all outcome categories. That is, depression scores, as well as other outcomes (automatic thoughts, emotional distress, serotonin and norepinephrine levels) significantly and similarly changed from pre- to post-intervention, and there were no between-group differences at post-intervention.

3.3 Description of an REBT Intervention for MDD in Children and Adolescents – A Patient Guide

3.3.1 Aims of this Guide

This material is intended to help you learn interesting things about depression signs and symptoms, and, most importantly, teach you various skills to use for managing your depressive symptoms and other related difficulties. The skills you're going to learn are rooted in what we call Rational Emotive Behavioral Therapy (REBT), a form of therapy designed to help you understand and manage your emotions and behavior by means of a healthy thinking style. By reading this manual, you'll learn about your habitual thinking style and how to modify it to be less depressive, more energetic, and more willing and successful in dealing with life difficulties.

3.3.2 What Is Depression?

Depression is a serious health problem that impacts every aspect of your life – how you feel, think and act. It is more than the common turmoil and uncertainty, or moodiness that most youth face, especially during their transition to adolescence and adult life. Depression goes beyond sadness, disappointment, dissatisfaction, bad mood or bad days. It's natural to feel sad, down or discouraged at times. We all feel these human emotions, when we face difficult situations, like family tensions, school problems or quarrel with a dear one. When healthy, emotions – either positive or negative – signal that something has changed in our environment and help us to successfully manage the change. However, when unhealthy, emotions are overwhelming, last unjustifiably long and hinder our adaptation. For example, healthy negative emotions help us to take a break, reevaluate the options and make our choices. Typically, they don't last long. By contrast, unhealthy negative emotions hinder our ability to face the difficult situation, make the situation worse, by creating additional problems, and may give us the impression that there is no way out.

The difference between depression and sadness lies specifically in their healthy/unhealthy features: while depression is an unhealthy emotion, sadness is a healthy one.

The table below illustrates the differences between sadness and depression. To illustrate the differences, we're going to use a hypothetical situation in which you're mocked by peers because something you wear. We'll going to call this situation "social rejection", because most of teens feel rejected when others make fun of them.

3.3.2.1 Situation: Social Rejection

Sadness/disappointment	Depression
We assess the situation realistically ("they make fun of me right now")	We tend to overestimate the badness of the situation ("they mock me as I am the last human being on the earth")
We think this is an unwelcome situation ("I'd wished they didn't")	We think this situation is unacceptable/ shouldn't exist ("they shouldn't do this ever!")

(continued)

Sadness/disappointment	Depression
We assess realistically our ability to manage the challenge properly ("maybe I can tell them I don't like it? / maybe I can ask them how they liked the last movie? / maybe I can laugh with them, then move forward?")	We feel powerless and think we cannot do anything to change the situation ("I'm only a victim, there's nothing I can do to change this miserable situation.")
We don't think they're right to make fun of us	We think they're right to make fun of us
We don't remember lots of occasions when others rejected us, neither we think this is our common experience with people	We remember lots of occasions when others rejected us and tend to think that people typically reject us
We don't think mean of us	We think mean of us ("I deserve it, I'm a miserable, stupid fool")
We remember that the situation won't last forever	We don't think things will be different in future ("this isn't going to change ever")
We tend to manage the situation properly	We tend to avoid social situations
We approach constructively the challenge	We tend to think over and over again on that situation, being mentally "blocked"; we feel overwhelmed
We're able to resolve/diminish the problem	We cannot think of viable solutions and don't get to test any possible solution
We're still able to enjoy other aspects of our life and treasure relationships with others	We're unable to enjoy other aspects of our life, to have meaningful relationships or to properly concentrate to other things

Importantly, depression is not experienced the same by everyone. Some teens may persistently feel very down, may think down of themselves, and try to avoid social contexts. Some may feel restless and particularly irritable without any clear reason. Others may feel always fatigued and with low levels of energy, prefer to sleep all the time, or use their smartphone as much as they can. Some may refuse food, because they lost their appetite, while others may eat excessively, especially sweets. Other signs and symptoms may include hopelessness, anger or hostility, tearfulness or frequent crying, withdrawal from friends and family, loss of interest in activities and poor school performance. Some manifest changes in eating or sleeping patterns, feel worthless and guilt, lack enthusiasm and motivation and are extremely sensitive to criticism. Others may report unexplained aches and pains, and even thoughts of death or suicide.

Anyways, depression is by no means a sign of weakness, insufficiency or worthlessness, neither something that disappears if the person strives enough. Depression is very damaging if left untreated over time. However, there is help and there is treatment. You're not supposed to fight by yourself with depression.

Things to remember

- ***Depression is a health problem;*** is different from sadness is that depression hinders our adaptation while sadness promotes it
- ***Signs and symptoms may differ from person to person, but they are persistent and disturbing***
- ***There is treatment and hope!***

3.3.3 *What Is Rational Emotive Behavior Therapy (REBT)?*

REBT is a treatment developed by a psychiatrist named Albert Ellis in 1955. This man observed that is not the situation that make us feel a specific emotion, but rather the way we perceive situations. In other words, he showed that the way we think about a situation make us feel in a certain way. Remember the social rejection situation described above? You saw that in the same very situation one can feel sadness (or disappointment) while other can feel depression. What makes the differences? Mainly, the way people think about the situation: if you think that something should (or shouldn't) happen necessarily, and if you think low of yourself, you're likely to feel depressed; on contrast, if you think that something unwanted just happened, and don't blame yourself/aren't harsh to yourself, you'll feel sadness.

Albert Ellis said that there are two ways of thinking about a situation:

1. ***The rational way*** – which sees the situation realistically, look for evidence supporting thoughts, and try to figure out a logical conclusion, promoting a feasible solution
2. ***The irrational way*** – which exaggerate the badness of a situation, accept negative thoughts without questioning, and arrive at distorted, wrong conclusion, which hinder the identification and implementation of feasible solutions

Albert Ellis' most important contributions to the understanding of human emotions was his proposal that emotions can be classified not only as positive and negative, but also as healthy and unhealthy. He said that emotions are not good or bad because they are positive or negative! Both positive and negative emotions can be useful (healthy, or good) or useless (detrimental, unhealthy, bad). How is that possible? Let's see first how a positive emotion (which is pleasant, desirable) can be unhealthy. Imagine that your friend is super happy, full of energy and very self-confident. Consequently, he decides to have a drink, and then drive crazy on the motorway. He feels high! But this emotion, although positive, is not healthy for him, isn't it? He could have an accident, he could hurt himself and others. You see? Positive emotions aren't always good: when they put you at risk or create problems to you, they're unhealthy.

The same is with negative emotions: they can help you be in control of your life or they can hamper your ability to look forward for solutions to reach your goals. Read again the table above. You see? It's healthy to feel sadness/disappointment – it prevents you of being emotionally hurt further. It's like putting your hand on something hot: you feel the pain and act. Pain is unpleasant (and so is sadness), but what if you wouldn't feel the pain?

By contrast, it's unhealthy to feel depression. Why? It makes you feel worse and hinder your ability to change the bad situation or to depart from it. It's like you'd felt the pain perpetually, even if you took your hand off from the hot surface long time ago; or it's like you would feel terrible pain but couldn't think and hadn't the energy to take your hand off from the hot surface.

Simply put, negative emotions are unhealthy when they last unreasonably long, affect your performance, and impede your capacity to enjoy experiences or to reach your goals.

Albert Ellis proposed that ***healthy emotions are underpinned by rational thinking, while unhealthy ones are underpinned by irrational thinking***. REBT teaches you how to identify and actively combat your irrational thinking to accommodate a rational world view, which makes you feel better both emotionally and physically, and adopt healthier behaviors. To that end, REBT makes use of different strategies:

1. Cognitive strategies – i.e., ways of change irrational thinking to alleviate your mood
2. Behavioral strategies – i.e., ways of promoting healthy behaviors
3. Emotional strategies – i.e., ways of combating negative thoughts by means of emotion (like emotions primed by humor, music, poetry etc.)

Things to remember
- **REBT was invented by Albert Ellis; it stands for Rational Emotive Behavior Therapy**
- **There are two main types of thinking: rational and irrational**
- **Emotions are not only positive and negative, they can be healthy or unhealthy; healthy emotions are supported by rational thinking, while unhealthy ones are supported by irrational thinking**
- **REBT makes use of cognitive, behavioral and emotional strategies to combat depression**

3.3.4 Managing Depression with Cognitive Strategies: The ABC of Depression

You already know by now that is not the situation that makes you depressed but is the way you think about the situation (remember the social rejection situation we discussed above). The way you THINK make you feel certain emotions and act in certain ways. The graphic below illustrates this:

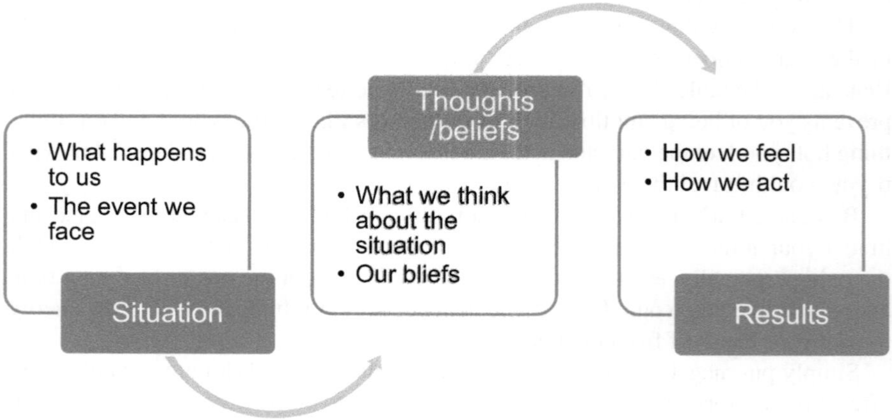

Situations are called also ***A**ctivating events*. The thinking process is referred also as ***B**eliefs*. And Results are called also ***C**onsequences*. Therefore, **the ABC of depression** is as simple as this: *is not the **A**(ctivating event), but the **B**(beliefs) you hold that give you certain **C**(onsequences) in terms of how you feel and act.* ***A – B –C***

Let's look at an **example**:

Michael and Jonathan are colleagues. They both gave a math test, and both got poor marks. When the marks have been announced, Michael reacted with sadness and disappointment. He told his parents about the mark, tried to understand what happened, and conclude that it was the less effort he put on math during the last semester. He saw the situation like this: "*I don't like at all I've got this mark. I'm disappointed, but I have to accept the reality. If I got this mark, it means that my performance wasn't satisfactory. I can accept this and I'm going to put more effort to improve it, although math is not my strength*". Jonathan, on the other hand, felt guilt and depressive. He avoids social contacts and spend most of the time using his smartphone (he plays games). He thinks like this about the situation: "*I shouldn't get this mark! It's only my fault! This is only a confirmation that I'm nothing than a worthless looser, the most stupid human being on Earth!*"

You see, both Michael and Jonathan faced the same situation, the same activating event. However, one of them felt sadness and disappointment, while the other one get depressed. Their beliefs/thoughts about the situations and about themselves made the difference!

Now, knowing this, how can we control the depression? By controlling the beliefs, right? But how's that possible?

First, let us show you **the main irrational/detrimental beliefs**: once you can recognize them, it will be easier to combat them.

Albert Ellis told us about **four main beliefs**:

1. **Demandingness (DEM)**: belief that things should necessarily go certain ways (e.g., "I must succeed, I don't accept anything else"; "They should love me."; "I must be happy.")

   • Why is this irrational?

   (i) It's rigid, it doesn't admit any exception or situation that might contradict our expectations
   (ii) It doesn't reflect the reality: reality is not like we tell it should be
   (iii) It doesn't help us: when things don't come as we expect them, this belief make us feel unhealthy emotions and act unproductively

   • What's the alternative? ***Flexible preferences***: "I wish to be successful and I'm doing my best, but I accept that there is no guarantee I'll achieve it."

   (i) It's flexible, it admits that not everything depends on us and there are situations when, despite our efforts, we don't obtain what we want
   (ii) It does reflect the reality: it expresses our wish without demanding that the reality should conform to it
   (iii) It helps us to assume the responsibility for what we can control

2. **Global evaluation (GE)**: belief that one is in a certain way, based on certain behaviors (e.g., "I missed the class, I'm a stupid fool."; "I won the contest, I'm a genius"; "I hurt her, I'm a miserable.")

   - Why is this irrational?

   (i) It's inflexible: it leads to a generalization based on an isolated incident
   (ii) It doesn't reflect the reality: the reality is that we are more complex beings, doing wrongs and rights all the time
   (iii) It doesn't help us: it makes us feel guilty, doesn't help us to identify and resolve the true problem

   - What's the alternative? ***Unconditional acceptance*** of a person, while striving to improve/change undesirable behaviors

   (i) It's flexible: it assesses specific behaviors, it doesn't label the person
   (ii) It does reflect the reality: the reality is some of our behaviors are performant, while others aren't
   (iii) It helps us: we can identify undesirable behaviors and reflect on how we can remediate them

3. **Frustration Intolerance (FI):** belief that one cannot stand something unpleasant (e.g., "I cannot stand my parents talking like this."; "I cannot stand my peers making fun of me.")

   - Why is this irrational?

   (i) It's inflexible: it doesn't accept the possibility that we could stand something we don't like
   (ii) It doesn't reflect the reality: the reality is we can stand (at least for a while) anything even if we don't like it (don't like ≠ I cannot stand)
   (iii) It doesn't help us: it can demotivate us to try to change anything and promote escape and avoidance

   - What's the alternative? ***Frustration tolerance***: "I can stand it and it deserves the effort."

   (i) It's flexible: it admits that even it's unpleasant or difficult, we can stand it, at least for a while
   (ii) It does reflect the reality: the reality is we don't like it, but can stand it
   (iii) It does help us: it can motivate us to make a change, to make the things more comfortable/supportable

4. **Awfulizing/Catastrophizing (AWF):** belief that something unpleasant that happened is the most terrible thing that could have happened (e.g. "This is awful, there's nothing worse."; "If I break with my boyfriend, it's horrific.").

   - Why is this irrational?

   (i) It's inflexible: it doesn't admit that there is always a hierarchy of bad things; it considers something 100% bad (it doesn't see nuances)

(ii) It doesn't reflect the reality: there is always something worse that we didn't consider (for example, by comparing a bad mark with a serious car accident, we can see the bad mark isn't the worst thing; and we can always compare the remaining thing – the car accident – with even a worse thing, and so on)
(iii) It doesn't help us: when catastrophizing, it's difficult to assume responsibilities; we tend to distract ourselves and postpone important things; we may see no solution

- What's the alternative? ***Non-catastrophizing***, or realistically evaluating a negative event as "negative/bad" (but not worst): "It's unpleasant/bad that this is happening."

(i) It's flexible: it doesn't consider something 100% bad necessarily, but recognize the unwanted/unpleasant aspects
(iv) It does reflect the reality: we can say about something it's bad, but recognize we haven't access to all the bad things in the world, so we cannot say it's the worst (and probably it isn't)
(v) It does help us: we focus on what we can do instead of distracting ourselves or postpone action

All these irrational beliefs may be involved in depression, but the combination of the first two (DEM and GE) is especially potent. Look again at how Jonathan perceive the situation he faces. Can you identify the DEM and GE? Write them below:

DEM : ……………………………………………………………………………
GE : ……………………………………………………………………………

Things to remember

- **The ABC of depression: between an activating event (A) and its consequences (C) is always a B (beliefs)!**
- **Irrational beliefs lead to unhealthy emotions and behaviors, while rational ones are associated with healthy emotions and behaviors**
- **There are four main types of irrational beliefs (with their rational counterparts): demandingness (DEM; its alternative: flexible preferences); global evaluation (GE; its alternative: unconditional acceptance of self); frustration intolerance (FI; its alternative: frustration tolerance); and awfulizing/catastrophizing (AWF; its alternative: non-catastrophizing)**
- **DEM + GE are especially powerful in generating depression**

3.3.4.1 How Can One Turn Irrational Beliefs into Rational Ones?

The answer is: through practice! If you can recognize the irrational beliefs behind your unhealthy emotions, you can challenge them and turn them into rational ones. This way, you can influence how you feel/you can change your emotions.

To **challenge (or dispute) irrational beliefs**, we can use the following questions:

- How flexible is this belief? Does it permit exceptions? What if this is an exception?
- What's the evidence supporting my belief? Does it reflect the reality? How?
- How logical is my belief? How did I conclude that things stay like this?
- Does it help me? How?

Once you successfully analyzed/disputed your irrational beliefs, what you need is to formulate alternative beliefs. Ask yourself: "What belief is more flexible, realistic, logical and helpful?", then formulate alternatives. Last, but not least, you need to act in accordance with your new, rational beliefs. By doing this, your emotions will be changed, and so will be your behavior.

Let's take an **example**:

Lucia found out that her mother has cancer. She isn't popular at school and has been often bullied as she's a gipsy and doesn't know her biological father. Despite all these, she used to be a good student. But now she's done: she's feeling extremely depressed and hopelessness. Her school performance dropped dramatically, she socially withdrew even more (now she isn't chatting with her only two friends at school) and cries often. She thinks like this: "*Life is not fair! It should be fair, for God's sake! Why should I face all of these? I cannot stand them! It's simple horrible! And now, my mother... Oh, my God, it's awful... how can she have cancer? No... that's too much, I cannot stand it. Maybe all of this is because of me. However, I have been always nothing but a looser. I'm just a stupid gipsy girl. And maybe my mother got ill because of me. Maybe if she hadn't had me, she was healthy now. It's only my fault! I wish I wasn't born!*"

- Can you identify Lucia's depressive symptoms?
- Can you identify her irrational beliefs?
- Can you dispute her irrational beliefs?
- Can you suggest some alternative, rational beliefs for Lucia?
- How would Lucia act differently if she had alternative, rational beliefs?

(after trying to offer you responses, you can compare them with those in the *Answer Key* at the end of this guide)

Things to remember

- **Irrational beliefs can (and should) be disputed and replaced by rational ones; this will causally influence emotion and behavior**
- **Disputation needs a lot of PRACTICE: more often, better**
- **The proof of a correct disputation of rational belief is you genuinely give up to the old belief, adopt the new one as truthful, and change your behavior accordingly**

3.3.4.2 Fighting Back Depression with Behavioral Techniques

When depressed, most people don't feel like they can or want to do things – they have low levels of energy and are totally demotivated. Usually, they tend to procrastinate all activities they can procrastinate, in the idea that they'll do those when they'll be in the right mood. The problem is "the right mood" is increasingly far away every day. What is the explanation for this? When depressed and feeling low, one feels like having no resources for doing anything. By doing nothing, his/her mood go increasingly low, and one feels even more like doing nothing. Practically, when depressed people isolate themselves and avoid activities and this just maintains or worsens their depression. It's like a vicious circle (see below):

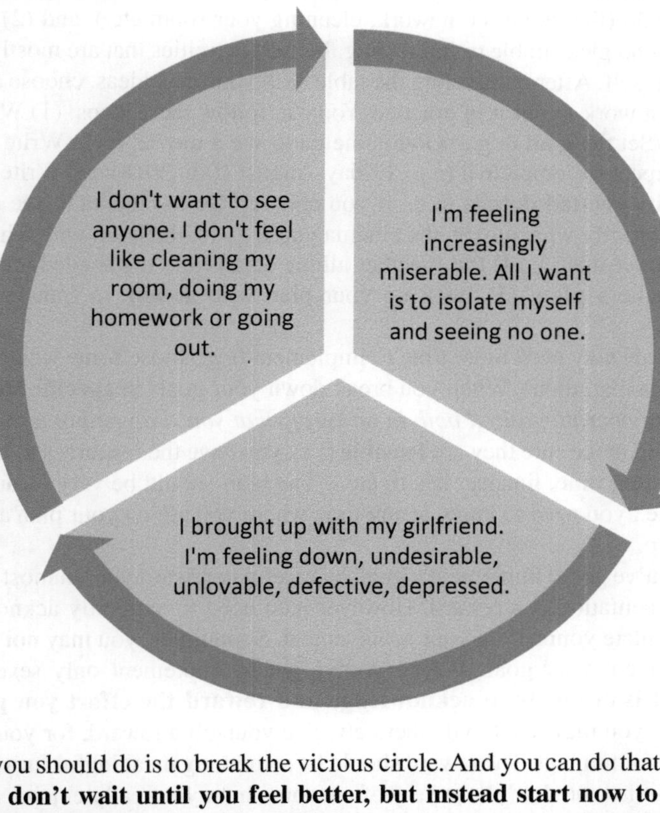

What you should do is to break the vicious circle. And you can do that only if you **decide to don't wait until you feel better, but instead start now to do things, even you don't feel like**. By doing things, you'll start to feel a little bit better, and that will fuel you with energy to do the next thing, while depression will fade away.

Let's see how you can break the vicious circle.

The first behavioral strategy is called "*behavioral activation*". It's about choosing activities, setting goals, pursuing them, while rewarding yourself for completing your goals. However, choosing activities and setting goals may seem overwhelming when depressed. As you may need a framework, you can start here: let's look at the table below.

Area	Suggested activities
Leisure & hobbies	Go to cinema to see a movie; read a novel; knit a scarf; plant a tree; listen to music
Health and personal care	Loose weight 3 kg; run 10 km; ride the bike once a week; go out for a walk
Family and friends	Spending time (and enjoying it) with family; going out with friends; visit grandparents
Academic	Doing my homework; studying about a specific subject; working for a practical project

You can complete the table with your own ideas, both in the "Area" entry, as in the "Suggested activities" entry. Think especially about (1) those activities you are expected to do (like doing homework, cleaning your room etc.), and (2) activities you once found pleasurable or interesting. Include activities that are mostly controllable by yourself. After completing the table with your own ideas, choose at least an activity, then work to put it in practice. You can follow these steps: (1) Write down the activity/Set the **goal** (e.g., "Go to cinema to see a movie"); (2) Write down the **date** you expect to complete it (e.g., Friday, August 10th, 2018); (3) Write down the other **activity-related details** (e.g., if you choose "Go to cinema to see a movie", you should specify what movie, the cinema you'll go to, the hour, with whom you'll go, the ticket cost etc.); (4) Put together all the details and the needed intermediary steps, to make a **plan**; (5) Back up your plan with **action**, to transform it into **reality**.

Some goals may need more time to implement (e.g., loose some weight, or train for running a marathon). When you break down your goals in **specific steps**, make sure they are *operationalized both in terms of what you'll do and in terms of when you'll do*, and make sure they are **feasible** (i.e., you have the resources to implement them, including time, finance, health etc.). The plan should be very clear and easy to follow, i.e., you need to know at any time where you are on your plan and what's the next step.

Once you've got to implement a goal, be careful to reward you. In most cases, the goal implementation is a reward. However, you need to explicitly acknowledge it and congratulate yourself on your achievement. Sometimes, you may not be able to fully implement your goal. Maybe you've got to implement only several steps. However, **it is crucially to acknowledge and reward the effort you put in**. At those times, you may need to deliberately give yourself a reward, for your genuine effort and commitment. The reward should be something meaningful for you, something you desire and don't have very often, something you really enjoy.

And, if you didn't succeed, don't give up! You can try again, you can look for help, you can try to discover what you can improve in your plan or revise your plan to make things more attainable for you.

After succeeding to implement a specific activity (you can begin with very simple ones, like "have lunch between 13:00 and 13:30"), you should plan your daily activities, Importantly, **breaks and pleasurable activities should be intertwined**

in your daily program. Why? Because you need to "refuel your batteries". If you do only what you're supposed to do, and this become increasingly tiring for you, you are at risk at entering the vicious cycle we discussed earlier.

Also, take care to **set realistic goals** every day. Remember, there are a limited number of things you can do during a day. Don't overschedule!

Another practical suggestion for behavioral activation (suggestion that can be used together with the one described above) is to monitor your behavior; just write down, at specific times during the days, what you do and how you feel right then. This way you can have a general picture of the behaviors you do daily, and how they influence your mood. Another variation is to choose a specific behavior you want to make more often (or, on the contrary, you want to get rid of). Just begin to monitor that behavior – write down how many times per day you do that specific behavior. By just monitoring, you can influence its occurrence (the behavior will tend to go in the direction you desire, i.e., increase or decrease in frequency).

While implementing behavioral techniques, be aware of irrational beliefs that could undermine your efforts (e.g., "It's too hard. I can't succeed."), and, if needed, dispute them before going further with behavioral techniques.

Things to remember

- **Don't wait to feel better to do useful things! Just do them, THEN you'll feel better!**
- **Set a goal (i.e., an activity written down with a date), break it in specific steps (set milestones), plan, back up your plan with action. Reward yourself!**
- **Plan and monitor your daily program. Take care to include breaks and pleasurable activities. Aim a balanced daily program, not an overloaded one.**

Another category of behavioral strategies designed to fight back depression are **distraction techniques**. They are intended to give your mind a break from negative, repetitive thoughts. To distract yourself, you can: (1) do something that "absorb" yourself (play your favorite musical instrument, sing a song, dance, watch a movie or read something "absorbing"); (2) imagine a pleasant place – maybe a place you visited, want to visit or just an imaginary spot. Put lots of details, make the image as vivid as possible; (3) take a break and go out for a walk: focus on what you hear, see, touch, smell, taste. Be totally aware of your senses and try to describe as detailed as possible how you perceive reality through your senses. (4) visualize a "STOP" sign, the end of a path, or an infinite wall, and imagine it's impossible to go further with your negative thinking.

There is one more category of intervention techniques used in the REBT treatment of depression: namely, ***emotive techniques***. These techniques are aimed to combat negative thinking by means of emotion. What does this mean? It means you'll make yourself feel certain emotions, that help you to gain a new understanding of the situation. For example, you can use humor, to make fun of your ridiculous, irrational beliefs. You can transform them into characters and can imagine a charade. You can write songs/poems/stories, or create metaphors about your experiences, thoughts, feelings, behaviors. However, one of the most powerful emotive technique is giving yourself the chance of living intentionally ridiculous experiences. This strategy is called "shame-attack exercise" and consists in exposing yourself to situations you previously believed that are unbearable and you can't tolerate. The goal is to give yourself a sense of experiencing unconditional self-acceptance despite ridiculous behavior. For example, Albert Ellis told he used to be very anxious in initiating a date with a girl; so, he choose to deliberate ask every girl he met to go out with him, no matter how ridiculous this request was. Of course, he received lots of refuses, but at the same time he experienced lots of emotions, until he was capable to look detached to the whole idea of asking for a date and being refused. Other examples of shame-attack exercise may be the following: go in front of an important building having a huge outside clock, and keep asking passers-by what's the hour; or say something unexpected or redundant in a public place (like announcing with a loud voice the next station in a tram, or saying something evident like "I have an important announce: tomorrow is Friday"). However, **before choosing and implementing any shame-attack exercise, it's very importantly to discuss it with your therapist** – as any shame-attack exercise implies challenging a minor social norm which shouldn't have a major impact on your social life but expose you to strong emotions you normally fear. You need to prepare a shame-attack exercise in advance with your therapist to remain safe, be able to manage the emotion you're going to experience and integrate the experience to consolidate your rational beliefs.

Answer Key

(1)

Jonathan's DEM: "I **<u>shouldn't</u>** get this mark!"

Jonathan's GE: "I'm nothing than a **worthless looser**, the **most stupid human** being on the Earth"

(2)

Lucia's depressive symptoms: she is feeling depressed and is hopeless; she seems to isolate herself and avoid her friends; her school performance worsen; she cries often

Lucia's irrational beliefs:

- DEM: Life should be fair.
- GE: I have been nothing but a loser, a stupid gipsy girl.
- AFW: It's horrible! It's awful my mom has cancer.
- LFT: I cannot stand them! It's too much, I cannot stand the fact that my mom has cancer.

Disputing Lucia's irrational beliefs:

- Who says life should be fair? Always? Are there exceptions? Isn't this belief a rigid, inflexible one? What are the proofs that life should be fair (how it is in reality?) Does it help me to think like this?
- Yes, I'm gipsy, but does this make me an inferior human being? What's the evidence I'm stupid? Have I had any performant behaviors? Have I ever done a smart thing? What about the thing that I'm loving so much my mother? What about my school performance? What's the evidence I'm always (with no exception) a loser? Is there any piece of evidence against it? How did I get to the conclusion that, because my mom is ill, it's my fault? Is there any other possible explanation? How probable is that explanation? Can I ever find it out if it's truly my fault? Does this style of thinking help me?
- Is there anything more terrible than my mom having cancer? What about having no access to treatment, nor to analgesics? What about being ill myself and not able to help her? Does it help me to think like this? How?
- What's the evidence I cannot stand it? Does it help me to think like that?

Alternative, rational beliefs for Lucia:

- Flexible preferences: I'd wished with my everything to have a better life, but I know and accept that I cannot control everything. I'm doing my best to have the best possible life.
- Unconditional self-acceptance: I'm a human being like anyone else. I'm equally worthy. Maybe I cannot do much, but I'm doing everything in my power for my mother. However, I'm not worthy because of that – that's only something good I'm doing.
- Non-awfulizing: It's very, very bad my mom got ill. It's such a painful situation for me and for her, but I'm aware that it isn't the worst thing in the world yet. We'll do everything in our power to fight cancer.
- Frustration tolerance: I don't like – actually I hate! – we must go through this. It's very difficult for both of us, but as we go through it, it seems we can stand it, at least for now.

How should Lucia act differently, based on her rational beliefs:

- She would look for solutions: she inquiries about treatment (what is involves, how long it is, what's the effect on her mother, how can she help her mother), ways of supporting her mom etc.
- She would encourage her mom
- She would speak about her pain with her best friends; she would look out for help if she isn't able to manage the emotional pain or to identify solutions
- She would be able to concentrate for her school work, given the time and resources she has
- She would cry less and feel confident she masters/controls her crying (and not the other way)

References

Arnkoff, D. B., Glass, C. R., & Shapiro, S. J. (2002). Expectations and preferences. In J. C. Norcross (Ed.), *Psychotherapy relationships that work: Therapist contributions and responsiveness to patients* (pp. 335–356). New York: Oxford University Press.

Beck, A. T., Rush, A. J., Shaw, B. F., & Emery, G. (1979). *Cognitive therapy of depression*. New York: Guilford Press.

Beck, J. S. (1995). *Cognitive therapy: Basics and beyond*. New York: Guilford Press.

Bernard, M., Vernon, A., Terjesen, M., & Kurasaki, R. (2013). Self-acceptance in the education and counseling of young people. In M. Bernard (Ed.), *The strength of self-acceptance*. New York: Springer.

Bernard, M. (2013). *The strength of self-acceptance. Theory, practice, and research*. New York: Springer.

Bieling, P. J., McCabe, R. E., & Antony, M. M. (2004). *Cognitive-behavioral therapy in groups*. New York: Guilford Press.

Clarke, G. N., Hornbrook, M. C., Lynch, F., Polen, M., Gale, J., Beardslee, W., ... Seeley, J. (2001). A randomized trial of a group cognitive intervention for preventing depression in adolescent offspring of depressed parents. *Archives of General Psychiatry, 58*(12), 1127–1134. https://doi.org/10.1001/archpsyc.58.12.1127

Clarke, G. N., Rohde, P., Lewinsohn, P. M., Hops, H., & Seeley, J. R. (1999). Cognitive-behavioral treatment of adolescent depression: Efficacy of acute group treatment and booster sessions. *Journal of the American Academy of Child and Adolescent Psychiatry, 38*, 272–279. https://doi.org/10.1097/00004583-199903000-00014

Clarke, G. N., Lewinsohn, P. M., Hops, H., & Seeley, J. R. (1990). *Adolescent coping with depression course*. Eugene, Ore: Castalia Press.

David, D. (2006). *Handbook of cognitive and behavioral psychotherapies* [Tratat de psihoterapii cognitive şi comportamentale]. Iasi: Polirom.

David, D. (2007). *Guide and clinical protocol of rational emotive behavior therapy for depression* [Ghid şi Protocol Clinic de Psihoterapie Raţional-Emotivă şi Comportamentală pentru Depresie]. Cluj-Napoca: Sinapsis.

David, D. (2015). Rational emotive behavior therapy. In R. L. Cautin & S. O. Lilienfeld (Eds.), *Encyclopedia of clinical psychology*. Hoboken, NJ: Wiley-Blackwell.

David, D., & Cramer, D. (2010). Rational and irrational beliefs in human feelings and psychophysiology. In D. David, S. J. Lynn, & A. Ellis (Eds.), *Rational and irrational beliefs in human functioning and disturbances*. Oxford: Oxford University Press.

David, O. A., & David, D. (2013). *The "PsyPills" app: Emerging modalities for applying CBT in real life*. Poster presented at EABCT Conference, Marrakech, September, 2013.

David, D., Szentagotai, A., Lupu, V., & Cosman, D. (2008). Rational emotive behavior therapy, cognitive therapy, and medication in the treatment of major depressive disorder: a randomized clinical trial, posttreatment outcomes, and six-month follow-up. *Journal of clinical psychology, 64*(6), 728–746. https://doi.org/10.1002/jclp.20487

Dilorenzo, T. A., Bovbjerg, D. H., Montgomery, G. H., Valdimarsdottir, H., & Jacobsen, P. B. (1999). The application of a shortened version of the profile of mood states in a sample of breast cancer chemotherapy patients. *British Journal of Health Psychology, 4*(4), 315–325. https://doi.org/10.1348/135910799168669

Dryden, W., & DiGiuseppe, R. (1990). *A primer on rational-emotive therapy*. Champaign, IL: Research Press.

Dryden, W., & Neenan, M. (2002). *Rational emotive behavioral group therapy*. London: Whurr Publishers.

D'Zurilla, T. J., & Nezu, A. M. (1999). *Problem-solving therapy: A social competence approach to clinical intervention* (2nd ed.). New York: Springer.

Ellis, A. (1987). A sadly neglected cognitive element in depression. *Cognitive Therapy and Research, 11*(1), 121–145.
Ellis, A. (1994). *Reason and emotion in psychotherapy* (re. ed.). Secaucus, NJ: Birch Lane.
Ellis, A. (2013). The value of a human being. In M. Bernard (Ed.), *The strength of self-acceptance* (pp. 65–72). New York: Springer.
Ellis, A., & Dryden, W. (1997). *The practice of rational emotive behavior therapy*. New York: Springer Publishing Company.
Eskin, M. (2012). *Problem solving therapy in the clinical practice*. London: Elsevier.
Hamilton, J. L., Strange, J. P., Kleiman, E. M., Hamlat, E. J., Abramson, L. Y., & Alloy, L. B. (2014). Cognitive vulnerabilities amplify the effect of early pubertal timing on interpersonal stress generation during adolescence. *Journal of Youth and Adolescence, 43*, 824–833. https://doi.org/10.1007/s10964-013-0015-5
Hien, D., Matzner, F. J., First, M. B., Spitzer, R. L., Williams, J., & Gibbon, M. (1994). *Structured clinical interview for DSM-IV childhood diagnoses (KID-SCID)*. Presented at the Biometrics Research presentation, New York.
Hollon, S. D., & Kendall, P. C. (1980). Cognitive self-statements in depression: Development of an automatic thoughts questionnaire. *Cognitive Therapy and Research, 4*(4), 383–395. https://doi.org/10.1007/BF01178214
Iftene, F., Predescu, E., Stefan, S., & David, D. (2015). Rational-emotive and cognitive-behavior therapy (REBT/CBT) versus pharmacotherapy versus REBT/CBT plus pharmacotherapy in the treatment of major depressive disorder in youth; A randomized clinical trial. *Psychiatry Research, 225*, 687–694. https://doi.org/10.1016/j.psychres.2014.11.021
Jacobson, E. (1929). *Progressive relaxation*. Chicago, IL: University of Chicago Press.
Knaus, W. J. (2012). *The cognitive-behavioral workbook for depression. A step-by-step program*. Oakland: New Harbinger Publications.
Kovacs, M. (1992). *Children's depression inventory*. North Tonawanda, NY: Multi-Health System.
Marcotte, D. (1996). Irrational beliefs and depression in adolescence. *Adolescence, 31*, 935–954.
Norcross, J. C. (2002). *Psychotherapy relationships that work: Therapist contributions and responsiveness to patients*. New York: Oxford University Press.
Rohde, P. (2011). Cognitive behavior therapy treatment for adolescents. In D. W. Springer, A. Rubin, & C. G. Beevers (Eds.), *Treatment of depression in adolescents and adults*. Hoboken: Wiley.
Solomon, A., Arnow, B. A., Gotlib, I. H., & Wind, B. (2003). Individualized measurement of irrational beliefs in remitted depressives. *Journal of Clinical Psychology, 59*(4), 439–455. https://doi.org/10.1002/jclp.10081
Verboom, C. E., Sijtsema, J. J., Verhulst, F. C., Penninx, B. W., & Ormel, J. (2014). Longitudinal associations between depressive problems, academic performance, and social functioning in adolescent boys and girls. *Developmental Psychology, 50*, 247–257. https://doi.org/10.1037/a0032547

Appendices

Appendix 1: ABCDEF Form

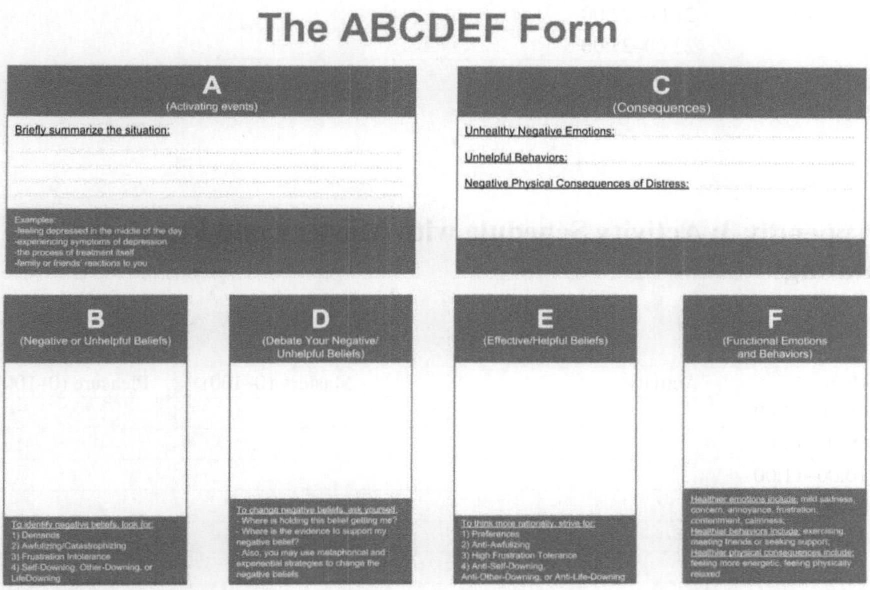
The ABCDEF Form

A
(Activating events)
Briefly summarize the situation:
Examples:
-feeling depressed in the middle of the day
-experiencing symptoms of depression
-the process of treatment itself
-family or friends' reactions to you

C
(Consequences)
Unhealthy Negative Emotions:
Unhelpful Behaviors:
Negative Physical Consequences of Distress:

B
(Negative or Unhelpful Beliefs)
To identify negative beliefs, look for:
1) Demands
2) Awfulizing/Catastrophizing
3) Frustration Intolerance
4) Self-Downing, Other-Downing, or LifeDowning

D
(Debate Your Negative/ Unhelpful Beliefs)
To change negative beliefs, ask yourself:
- Where is holding this belief getting me?
- Where is the evidence to support my negative belief?
- Also, you may use metaphorical and experiential strategies to change the negative beliefs

E
(Effective/Helpful Beliefs)
To think more rationally, strive for:
1) Preferences
2) Anti-Awfulizing
3) High Frustration Tolerance
4) Anti-Self-Downing, Anti-Other-Downing, or Anti-Life-Downing

F
(Functional Emotions and Behaviors)
Healthier emotions include: mild sadness, concern, annoyance, frustration, contentment, calmness;
Healthier behaviors include: exercising, meeting friends or seeking support;
Healthier physical consequences include: feeling more energetic, feeling physically relaxed

D. Cândea et al., *REBT in the Treatment of Subclinical and Clinical Depression*, SpringerBriefs in Psychology, https://doi.org/10.1007/978-3-030-03968-4

Appendix 2: Activity Schedule

Hour	Activity
08:00–09:00	
09:00–10:00	
10:00–11:00	
11:00–12:00	
12:00–13:00	
13:00–14:00	
14:00–15:00	
15:00–16:00	
16:00–17:00	
17:00–18:00	
18:00–19:00	
19:00–20:00	
20:00–21:00	
21:00–22:00	
22:00–23:00	
23:00–24:00	

Appendix 3: Activity Schedule with Mastery and Pleasure Ratings

Hour	Activity	Mastery (0–100)	Pleasure (0–100)
08:00–09:00			
09:00–10:00			
10:00–11:00			
11:00–12:00			
12:00–13:00			
13:00–14:00			
14:00–15:00			
15:00–16:00			
16:00–17:00			
17:00–18:00			
18:00–19:00			
19:00–20:00			
20:00–21:00			
21:00–22:00			
22:00–23:00			
23:00–24:00			

MIX
Papier aus verantwortungsvollen Quellen
Paper from responsible sources
FSC® C105338

If you have any concerns about our products,
you can contact us on
ProductSafety@springernature.com

In case Publisher is established outside the EU,
the EU authorized representative is:
Springer Nature Customer Service Center GmbH
Europaplatz 3, 69115 Heidelberg, Germany

Printed by Libri Plureos GmbH
in Hamburg, Germany